# Stitching Free

## Easy Machine Pictures

*by Shirley Nilsson*

C&T PUBLISHING

Unless otherwise noted, all photographs are by Ken Wagner, Seattle, Washington. The following photos in the Color Section are courtesy of Creative Quilting Publishing Co., Inc., New York, New York: Storytime; Christmas Angel; Wynken, Blynken, and Nod; Jane's Winter View; Della Robbia Wreath; A Is For Apple; Blue Gossamer Wings; Spring Song; and Shore Birds. Photo on page 36 is by Mark Lamoreaux. Two photos on page 45 are by Jerry Prout, Moscow, Idaho.

Illustrations around chapter heads and beside page numbers designed and sewn by Shirley Nilsson. All other illustrations drawn by Kristine Smith, The Woodlands, Texas.

Cover quilt designed and made by Shirley Nilsson, Bremerton, Washington, and photographed by Image West, Walnut Creek, California; cover typography by Gillian Johnson, Hanover, Maryland.

Editing by Louise Owens Townsend.

Technical editing by Elizabeth Aneloski.

Design and production coordination by Gillian Johnson, Merrifield Graphics, Hanover, Maryland.

Published by C & T Publishing, P. O. Box 1456, Lafayette, California 94549.

ISBN 0-914881-68-X

Library of Congress Cataloging-in-Publication Data

Nilsson, Shirley, 1930-
      Stitching free: easy machine pictures / by Shirley Nilsson.
    1st ed.
          p.   cm.
    Includes bibliographical references.
    ISBN 0-914881-68-X
    1. Fabric pictures.  2. Machine sewing. 3. Textile crafts.
    I. Title.
    TT751.N55      1993
    746.3—dc20               93-21483
                        CIP

"Catch a Falling Star" is by Paul J. Vance and Lee Pockriss (RCA Victor)
Singer Featherweight is a registered trademark of Singer Corporation.

Printed in the Hong Kong
First Edition

10    9    8    7    6    5    4    3    2    1

# Dedication

This book is dedicated to all of the children, beginning with my
three sons, Eric, Chris, and David, who through the years
have shared with me their art, their stories, and their feelings. All
of this was intertwined with enthusiasm, joy, humor, and love, and
has been a constant source of inspiration and delight.

# Acknowledgments

TO:     Jan Burns, Editor of *Creative Quilting,*
        for
        Believing and for those gentle prods.


TO:     All of my students through the years
        for
        Teaching me so very much


TO      All of the quilt groups where I have lived
        for
        Loads of friendship and support


TO:     Muffin the Cat
        for
        Inspiration and comic relief


TO:     Son David
        for
        Technical help and "I know you can!"


TO:     Chris and Jackie
        for
        Hours of computer aid and care


TO:     Husband George
        for
        All of the above…plus
        learning to use the computer
        so I was free to create
        in my handwritten comfort zone.

# Table of Contents

*Color Section begins on page 33.*

# Preface: How It All Began

How do you define "sewing machine"? For most of us, it is a very necessary piece of equipment that performs useful tasks related to sewing together pieces of fabric. To me, the sewing machine is that and much more—it is an artist's tool. I use my sewing machine as a pencil, a pen or a paintbrush—I use it as a drawing tool.

Years ago when newly married, my husband and I purchased a brand new state-of-the-art home sewing machine. The one we chose was a Singer Featherweight™—shiny black with intricate gold scroll designs. It sewed forward and backward only, no zigzag or fancy stitches. It was the basic Model T Ford of the home sewing world. Now, some 40 years later, my

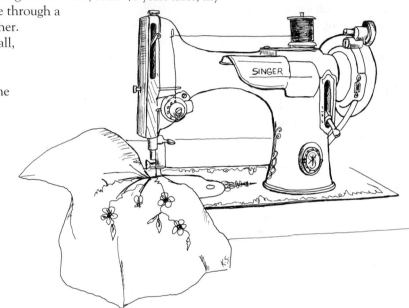

little machine and I have gone through a lot of living experiences together. When our three boys were small, I mended a lot—knees and elbows wore through on a regular basis. But I soon became bored with plain patches. I discovered that with my machine in the darning mode, I could make some wonderful free-flowing lines and shapes, and before long creative patches became my obsession. This was before patches were a fashion statement, so I got a lot of "Oh, Mother!" comments from my boys. Soon I discovered there was more to this new idea than just patching knees, and I began creating pictures. The children were delighted that I had found a new outlet, and I was really having fun. I have never looked back, and after 20 years of playing and experimenting and creating wondrous artworks, I am still discovering new possibilities.

I have added a new "computer" sewing machine to my sewing room, but my old friend Featherweight and I continue to produce all of my artwork. At the urging of many friends, I have written this book so that I can share with you my love of free-stitch machine drawing. Because my machine has no zigzag capability, my technique has developed using only straight stitch in a free-motion mode.

This book will show you how to use your sewing machine, whatever model it is, as a drawing tool. You'll learn how to use fabric pieces for color and texture and how to create your own lovely personal expressions in fabric. No previous drawing skills are needed. Just as a child learns to use a crayon to draw, you can learn to use your machine to draw on fabric. I also want to help you unlock that creative spirit that is within us all—let it bubble out—and allow you to create beautiful fabric art that is uniquely yours.

I encourage you, whatever your ability level, to discover, enjoy, and develop the skill of drawing with your sewing machine. I will lead you through the learning steps, always encouraging the development of your confidence in creative designing. You will explore ideas and approaches for incorporating this new drawing skill into your ongoing fabric projects, and you will be introduced to a wealth of new and exciting possibilities. Whether you are interested in fabric art pictures, quiltmaking, clothing, household fabrics, fabric sculpture or fabric surface design, this machine drawing technique can add a new excitement to your art and be an excellent vehicle to begin a whole new creative direction.

# Introduction: What Is It All About?

The sewing machine is a wonderful and indispensable tool for our sewing tasks, but have you ever considered it as a drawing tool? Through the years sewing machine manufacturers have been constantly perfecting new and amazing functions for their machines. With the push of a button or the flick of a switch, you and your machine can make tidy, even stitches any length you want, create beautiful patterns and diagrams in unending sequence, and perform numerous amazing programmable functions. You merely feed the fabric into the machine and all of this happens automatically.

Now I am going to suggest that you look at your sewing machine in a whole new way. Forget all of those wonderful mechanical capabilities for the moment and think of the machine's basic function: making a stitch through fabric. A series of stitches form a line on the fabric—now your machine becomes a line drawing tool. To create nice smooth free-flowing lines, you do not want to stop and turn the fabric when you change direction, so you need to eliminate the automatic feed action and take over that function yourself. Now, you are in control—a heady feeling.

If you don't move the fabric, the needle will go up and down in one spot, eventually forming a large lump of thread. If you move the fabric slowly, you will make tiny little stitches close together. If you move the fabric quickly, you will make long, gallumping stitches. You control the stitch length. You are also in control of the direction of the line of stitches, and you can make it straight or in zigs or zags or circles—any direction you want. This is your new drawing tool.

Have you watched children being introduced to crayons and paper? Usually they will try the crayon in one hand, then the other, try each end and even the middle and then discover that it can make marks on the paper—different kinds of marks. They are totally enthralled with the experience, savoring each moment. This trying and experiencing is the best way to become acquainted with your sewing machine as a drawing tool.

You should try several approaches and decide what you and your machine enjoy doing together. If you go into this with a sense of adventure, in no time you and your machine will establish a comfortable relationship and you will be creating wonderful lines, shapes and textures all your own.

Have you noticed that when you try to follow a precise line or reproduce an exact shape that you become very tense and uncomfortable? This is very destructive to the learning experience. The secret of a rewarding learning time, just as 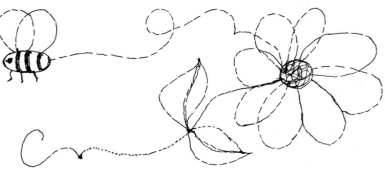 when you were a child, is to play freely—to scribble and doodle and enjoy the action and the new discoveries. Try not to allow thoughts of an end product to creep in—that will come later. Just play with the experience, allow yourself to get caught up in the moment, and move freely from one idea to the next. In this book you'll find plenty of motivation for beginning the free-stitching mode. I have created a page of doodles that will give you incentive and direction for launching into this new-skill learning experience. As you work through the process, you will soon discover how much fun it is to draw free-flowing lines and create textures and shapes using your sewing machine as a drawing tool. In no time you will develop confidence and discover the thrill and excitement of creating fabric art by stitching free!

Through the years of teaching machine drawing to a variety of skill levels, I have found that those who feel the most insecure about their pencil drawing skills are often the ones that are the most de-lighted with their new machine drawing abilities. When a new tool is used for the first time, everyone begins at the same level.

When this new machine drawing skill is yours, the fabric art world opens to a whole new set of possibilities. You can begin by adding fabric pieces for color and texture. In the spirit of this free-stitch method, I do not turn fabric edges under, but merely cut out the shape in the desired finished size, free-

or straight-stitch the edges to secure it and then, with a contrasting color of thread, define the shapes and draw in the details.

My objective is to help and encourage you to develop the skill, and then you will be ready to awaken your own inherent creative spirit. The following chapters and the Gallery of Soft Pictures are included to illustrate and explain some of the many ways that this new "drawing" skill can be used to enrich your own fabric creations.

It is important to play with the process and to become comfortable with the method and understand the various possibilities before you create a picture. Familiarity will allow you to keep that free spirit in motion.

When you are ready to start your first soft picture, Chapter 8 will give you the process step by step. In Chapter 9, I have included the directions for making three specific soft pictures. These are included to help you better understand the application of the process and to show how to create some special effects.

Have you noticed that in this explanation one word keeps cropping up? That word is free. I have mentioned free stitch, free-flowing lines, playful freedom, free edges—all while describing the method that I use. I would like to add one more freedom. Within each and every one of us is a creative spirit. It may be buried very deeply in some of us, but I assure you it is there. My hope is that when you learn this new drawing skill you will free the creative spirit within you, letting it flow out. Your life will be enriched immeasurably.

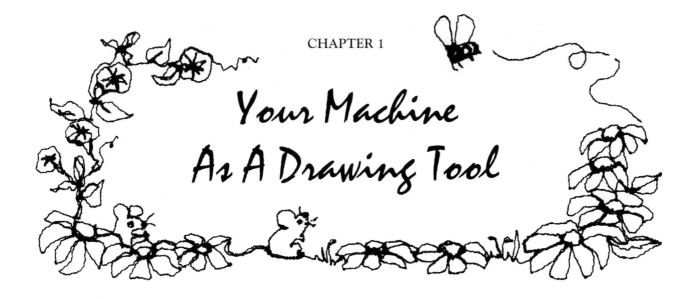

# CHAPTER 1

# Your Machine As A Drawing Tool

## The Darning Foot

What will you need to start this new adventure? A sewing machine that makes straight stitches (zigzag is not required), a capability to lower or cover the feed dog, and a spring-loaded darning foot. The foot should be designed to hold the fabric taut across the needle hole in the plate just long enough for the needle to go down through the fabric, loop with the bobbin thread and form the stitch. The foot should then lift up between stitches so you can move the fabric in any direction. The taut contact is necessary for most machines to form the stitch properly. These darning feet are designed with an arm that rests over or around the needle screw. Each time the needle lifts out of the fabric, the foot lifts at the same time and when the needle goes back down, so does the foot. The foot part is usually a small ring or U shape that successfully holds the fabric taut just at the needle insertion point. It is impossible to describe a single "jumper" or spring-loaded foot because each sewing machine manufacturer has a version unique to its machine, and these feet take many forms.

The design of each foot has changed several times through the years also compounding the difference. In the years I have been using a Singer machine, the company has produced at least four very different versions. Other machine manufacturers also have

changed the design of their darning foot to meet our current sewing needs. For my Featherweight, the original spring foot was just that—a gold-colored, spiral, cone-shaped coil spring—and these are still available. After that came a succession of shiny metal,

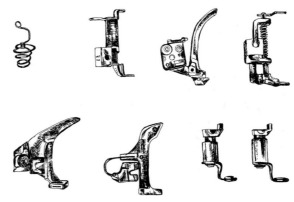

Presser Feet for the Sewing Machine

black metal, metal with a plastic foot, and all-clear plastic versions. The shape has varied with each change. The best plan for finding a foot for your machine is to consult your manual and/or your local machine distributor to find out what the most recent version of the spring-loaded darning foot is. If your machine does not have one, there are now some darning-foot models being produced that fit several machine styles. These are usually available through the suppliers for the major sewing machine manufacturers, or through fabric and sewing supply stores and catalogs. You will need to know if your machine has a short or long shank and how the feet attach to your machine. As the demand increases, the major machine companies are constantly upgrading the accessories, so check to see what is new. I find for my purposes that a

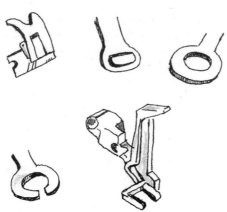

Closed and Open Presser Foot Shapes

small, round, closed loop of metal or a small clear plastic foot works well. The open U-shaped loop works, but will tend to get caught more easily on shaggy fabrics and deliberate thread loops.

## Adjusting Your Machine

Most machines today are capable of lowering the fabric feed mechanism. They used to call this "darning mode," but more recently refer to it as "adjusting for free stitch." If there is no way to lower the feed dogs, you still need a method of covering the teeth or raising the sewing bed level to where the fabric will not feed through. For some machines, a plate is available that covers the feed teeth. A plate with a small needle hole is an advantage in this method, so that thin fabrics will not have a tendency to be drawn down by the needle action. If your machine does not have a plate available, you can try making your own. Some of my students have had good results using a piece of rigid plastic. They punch or burn a small hole for the needle entry and then tape the plastic cover securely

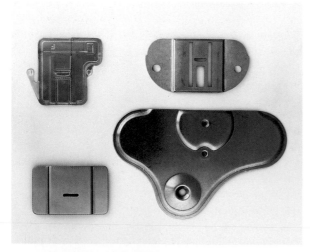

Cover Plates for Feed Dogs for the Sewing Machine

over the feed dog. You'll want to use a large-enough piece so that you have a smooth working surface free of snagging edges.

Sewing machines, I am convinced, have personalities all their own. My little machine and I have had many intense discussions through the years—some friendly, some not. We have worked through our differences and now know just what we can do together, and also what we enjoy doing together. While learning to use your machine as a drawing tool, you will become much more closely acquainted and probably you will develop an understanding and a feeling of mutual respect not experienced before. Instead of forcing the new experience and fighting the learning and re-learning, let your machine show you how to approach this new skill. Allow new things to happen and enjoy the differences. Soon you and your machine will become a team ready for a flight into a new world of experiences and possibilities.

Most of us are slaves to preconception. We decide what is going to happen and then are disappointed if it does not. Try to put yourself back to the exciting time of early learning. Immerse yourself in the experience and try not to preplan an end product. What you will gain is the excitement and fun of developing a new skill without performance pressure.

Have you ever noticed that if you try to follow a precise penciled line or a printed pattern that you become very tense and uptight? This reaction, although very normal, is not at all good for the spirit of freedom we are striving for in this new learning experience. So be sure to avoid pre-drawn lines—they are absolutely outlawed during the learning stage! Remember this is your kindergarten learning experience. Everyone starts out learning how to use a new tool at the same level. Just stay relaxed and enjoy this trial-and-error time of new experiences and new discoveries.

Another word of advice. What you are initially producing is your own private squiggles, lines, and

doodles. It is important at this stage not to be self-critical or to allow anyone else to be critical of your accomplishment and thus dampen your spirit of adventure.

You have now found and attached the spring-loaded foot and adjusted the feed mechanism so your sewing machine is ready to become a drawing tool. A question many students ask is "What about tension?" I hope that I have removed some of the "people tension" in the previous comments, but now we should address machine thread tension. This is an area where you may need to check your machine manual. Some machines will list a tension setting suggested for darning or free-motion straight stitch. For the learning process, most machines will work fine with the normal sewing tension setting. The tension settings of the top thread feed and the bobbin case and how they work together determine how the stitches look. With a balance of tension, ideally the threads will interlock within the fabric.

For the free-motion straight-stitch method, you want the top-surface stitches to be strong and clear. A slightly lowered (loosened) top tension may accomplish this. Try different settings until you are satisfied. Early on, my machine and I came to a firm agreement about tension setting. I don't mess with the tension, and it sews on contentedly forever. Trial and error will show you what works best for you and your machine.

## The Basic Action

You are ready now to learn how to draw with your sewing machine. Just as the first time you used a pencil or crayon to draw, this first-time experience requires time, experimentation, and trial to create lines on the fabric that go where you want them to go. To better understand the action involved, try this paper and pencil exercise:

Find a pencil and piece of paper and recruit a friend to help you. Have the friend hold the pencil vertically over the paper with the writing tip just

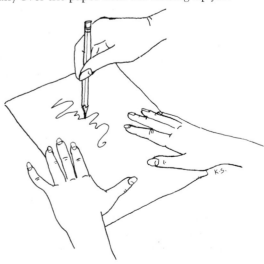

touching—enough to make a mark. The pencil is now the sewing machine needle and it will stay in one spot—it will not move. Now place your hands on the paper, palms down, one on each side of the pencil. Exerting light pressure with your hands, move the paper around under the pencil. Move from left to right, right to left, north, south, east, west, around in circles and back and forth. You are reproducing the drawing action. The key thing to understand is that the paper moves instead of the drawing tool. The way you move the paper determines the line direction. As someone who sews, you are used to the machine feeding the fabric through for you, either forward or reverse in predetermined, even-length stitches. That has now changed. You are in control, and how you move the fabric will decide the direction and the length of the stitches. You no longer need to turn the fabric to change the stitch line direction. The fabric can stay in the same north/south, east/west orientation and you can draw lines all over it. This is one of the old habits that is likely to take a little time to unlearn and re-program. With this sewing method, how quickly you move the fabric determines the length of the stitches. If you move the fabric quickly under the needle, you create long stitches. As you slow the fabric motion, the stitches become closer together and shorter or smaller. With no fabric movement, the stitches pile up, one on top of another, until the pile of stitches form a lump that breaks the needle.

The machine speed also figures in here. A fast machine speed with slow fabric movement creates lots of tiny stitches close together. A slower machine speed will give you more control while you are first beginning to learn the action. As you become more confident, a medium to rapid speed will give smoother more controlled lines. As you go, you will work out the best speed and motion for you. You are now in control. Your movement of the fabric determines what will happen, and what you create is entirely yours. Now—isn't that a heady feeling?

Line drawing with the sewing machine has a different quality than you get with other drawing tools. When you complete a part or finish a work with a pen you merely lift the pen from the paper and move it to the next starting point. With sewing machine drawing you will want to secure the thread ends at each start and stop so they won't pull out. Secure the threads by taking three or four stitches in place. You can then clip the threads off close to the fabric surface and continue to the next spot. You can also trail the threads to the next start and clip them off when you are finished. To do this take the stitches in place, lift the pressure foot lever, move to the new starting place, lower the foot lever, secure the threads again and continue sewing. If the trailing threads are in your way, simply clip them. What flows most easily is a continuous line. The fewer starts and stops you have, the freer the flow. For learning on your doodle cloth (see page 14), just keep going from one thought to another.

## Materials and Tools: What To Collect

For this first learning experience, find some medium to heavyweight fabric that has body or stiffness. Examples are unpainted canvas, cotton denim, sail cloth, broadcloth, trigger cloth, and cotton twill. Just as when you learn to drive a car, there are a lot of things to remember and coordinate. If you can eliminate some for the first experience, it will be more rewarding. With the heavier fabric, you will be able to concentrate on the basic method and the stitching action. Cut the selected fabric into manageable pieces that your machine arm will handle—9" x 12" works well.

Collect thread for the top that contrasts strongly with the fabric color so you can easily see what is happening. For example, with white fabric or canvas use a black thread. Use a matching bobbin thread. Regular sewing-weight thread is fine. You will want to have handy some small sharp scissors for clipping threads. I find the spring-action press-together thread nippers very useful for this. There are many varieties and styles available, so look for a pair that is sharp, accurate and works with one cut. Extra needles of a size to suit your thread and fabric will probably come in handy, too. You should be prepared to break a few needles—it goes with the learning process.

## How To Hold the Fabric

Do you remember the paper and pencil exercise? I find that I get the best control when I place my hands on

top of the fabric, one on each side and slightly in front of the needle. Because this is a small foot and you have a lot of things to focus on, you need to be extra careful not to get so engrossed that you sew through a finger! I

Thread Nippers

have a few scars that suggest times when I was distracted. With your hands in place, use a gentle downward pressure while you move the fabric. So that your arms don't tire quickly, you may want to rest your forearm on the table edge or rest your elbows there if you have a raised bed. You will soon discover what the most convenient pressure, placement, and hand action are for you.

Another reminder: You do not have to turn the fabric. You know the routine for regular sewing—needle down, stop action, foot up, turn fabric, foot down, continue sewing in new direction. All that is now thrown out the window. In free-stitch mode, you can now stitch in any direction, forming smooth curving lines without turning the fabric. You will be moving the fabric instead of turning it. To help you remember this new situation, make a mark on the top edge of your fabric piece and check yourself every now and then to see if it is still at the top. As you progress and learn the skill, you will develop your own comfortable hand placement and fabric action and direction. Remember that this is a whole new learning experience so forget traditional ways—break away and play—be free and open, and let the experience guide you.

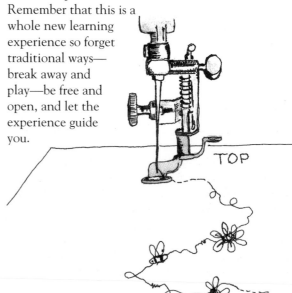

TOP

# CHAPTER 2

# Where To Start

Now you know what free-motion stitching is all about, and playtime is about to begin. In the checklist at the right you will find several things to check while preparing your equipment and beginning to draw with your sewing machine.

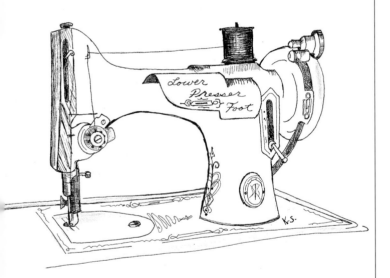

## Doodle Time

I have included the Doodle Page on page 14 just to help you get started. It should give you an idea of some things to try and how to progress with the learning. I hope it will launch you into a frenzy of your own exciting doodle patterns. Place the Doodle Page beside you and just follow along. Remember that your machine is your new drawing tool so don't draw lines with a pencil first. Just follow the ideas and draw with the machine stitches. You may feel really awkward at first, but just relax and enjoy the learning experience.

## A Checklist of Steps

1. **Darning Foot:** Attach the appropriate spring-loaded darning foot.
2. **Lower Feed Dog:** Lower or cover the feed mechanism.
3. **Tension:** Adjust tension where applicable—and relax.
4. **Speed Adjustment:** If your machine has a slow speed adjustment, it may be helpful at first to use it. As you progress try different speeds and hand-feed actions in combinations. You may discover that you want to just let-'er-rip.
5. **Thread:** Thread your machine with sewing thread in a color that shows up on your fabric.
6. **Fabric:** Cut a medium to heavy weight fabric approximately 9" x 12" and place on the machine bed. Mark one edge as TOP.
7. **Secure the Threads:** Insert the needle and pull the bobbin thread to the top. Holding both threads in the left hand, take two or three stitches in one spot. This will form a knot and the threads can then be clipped close to the knot.
8. **Lower the Foot Lever:** When using the spring darning foot, it is difficult to tell if the foot lever is lowered. Usually, if you are having problems with the thread looping and knotting, this is the culprit.
9. **Hands on Fabric:** Place hands comfortably on top of the fabric on each side of the needle. Use gentle downward pressure to move the fabric.

14

It is now time to start your engine! With the Doodle Page to guide you, secure the threads and start stitching.

Move the fabric up and over and down again, then down and up to draw curvy waves, and down and up for mountain peaks. Draw a triangle, a square, and any strange shape. Draw some loops, all sizes, and then some circles, squares, and rectangles, both alone and overlapped. Move the fabric quickly to charge across the cloth in great gallumping stitches. Then move the fabric slower and slower until you stop the fabric motion. This will make smaller and smaller stitches, and, finally a lump. Move on before you break the needle. Draw a small circle and fill it in to form a dot.

Draw some zigs and zags for mountain peaks, then zig and zag closer together to create grass and fur. Make the zigs uneven and scraggly, and then just scribble for awhile.

Draw some shapes and fill them in with these:

—ziggles: zigzag scribbles far apart and close together.

—squiggles: meandering lines that wander around to fill the space.

—cross hatching: lines that go back and forth one direction and then back and forth obliquely or at right angles to the first lines.

—spirals: start at the outside of a circle and spiral toward the center.

—contour spirals: lines that follow the outline of the shape and spiral into the center of the shape.

Draw some circles, then stitch around the outside six or more times until the center of the circle pops up in a pouffy "bloop."

Draw a flower and some leaves. Fill some parts with your favorite filling stitches.

Draw a bug or some other critter.

Write your name. To dot the "i," finish writing your name and secure the threads. Trail those threads back to the "i" and dot it with a few stitches in one place. Trim the trail away after removing fabric from the machine. Or, trail the threads again, secure them at the beginning, and draw a picture of yourself. Relax and play!

Now start with a new piece of cloth. Make your own discoveries. What happens when you go fast, go slow, move back and forth, or round and round in one spot? Keep in mind that this is playtime and learning-a-new-skill time. Creating great works of art will come later—now is the time for the fun and excitement of discovery! Play and experiment until the ideas are just bursting out and you have to try them!

# CHAPTER 3

# Adding Color and Texture

## The Process

Now that you are all charged up and comfortable with drawing lines and shapes it is time to add color and texture. Later, I will discuss different fabrics and their characteristics, but for now we will keep this free spirit flowing. The next step is appliqué with free-motion straight stitch. Appliqué is the action of applying one fabric piece to another, which I call the base fabric. There are many ways of doing this, both by hand and by sewing machine. Here we will use our new machine line-drawing skill to sew one piece to the other. In the spirit of easy application, I like to use fabric pieces with a cut edge. No tidy turned-under edges or covered-over edges—just raw-edged fabric cut to size and shape. There may be times you will want a tidier or turned under edge, but for the learning experience, stay loose and work with the raw-edged pieces. Continue to use your stiff fabric (canvas or denim, etc.) for the base, because it gives you a freedom to play with the method. So, grab another base piece (9" x 12") and a handful of small scraps and snippets of colorful cottons. (This gives you a wonderful justification for keeping all of those little pieces of fabric too small to use. Little pieces in haphazard shapes are perfect for this practice.)

Place a small piece on the base fabric and with free-motion straight stitch, sew it down around the edge. Once around is fine for this step—just enough to hold it in place. Don't be concerned if you miss a corner or go off the edge—go around again if you like. Now grab another color piece and sew it down—and a few more. Look at your tacked-down pieces and dream a little. Do the shapes make you think of some object? Maybe one looks like a cat or a flower or a tree—or just a blob.

Now draw over and "detail" the shapes using free-motion straight stitch to turn them into the objects you see. Or, if you prefer, just make interesting lines within and around the shapes. Draw freely both outside and inside the color shapes.

When I make my soft pictures, I tack down the pieces using a thread that matches or blends with the color of each piece. How well I tack it down depends on what kind of use it will get. Once around can be adequate for wall pieces, but clothing or quilt blocks will need to withstand wear and washing. A minimum

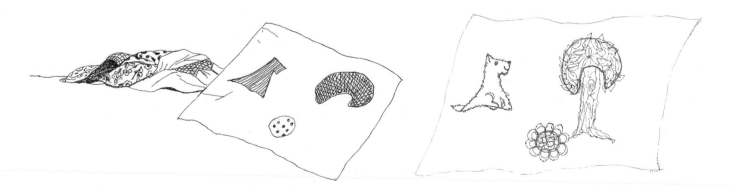

of three times around will ensure the edges are well secured and will reduce fraying. Once the pieces are tacked down, you can go back and freely play when you add the line-drawn details by machine in a contrasting thread color. I usually use black thread for this step. It works best not to try too hard to follow the outline of the shape when detailing. Your added fabric pieces or "patches" are blocks of color and texture that add interest, dimension, and shape to your artwork. Consider these shapes as background or as suggestions of form. When you draw over these shapes using contrasting colored stitches, you define the shapes and bring them into focus. If, when free stitching, you try to follow the contours or edges exactly, you will become tense and the free-flowing line quality will be disrupted. A creative on/off line that generally follows the shape but flows comfortably inside and outside of the edges is usually much more interesting visually. Relax and keep that freedom of motion flowing.

## Designing With Circles

Have you noticed, in nature, how many things can be translated easily into simple geometric shapes? Flowers can be circles, trees become triangles, and cows look like rectangles. Circles are probably the easiest shape to make into something. Just a few ideas are: leaves, stones, trees, birds, bird nests, apples, oranges, plums, sleeping cats, mice, bunnies, fish, shells, balls, bal-

loons, faces—the list is endless. Try this to get yourself started in creative designing: Cut out several circles of different sizes and colors, then make a picture. Place the circles on your base fabric and move them around, adding or subtracting, until an idea strikes you. Tack the circles down with matching or neutral thread.

With contrasting thread draw in details to make the circles into anything you want them to be.

## Bloops and Grumples

By now, you have probably discovered something else about sewing-machine drawing. If you sew around and around a circle lots of times, the center begins to dimple and soon you will have a wonderful "bloop."

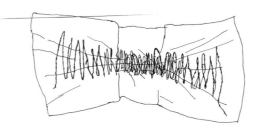

You can use these raised shapes or bloops to add texture and dimension to your pictures. If you sew around and around shapes many times, they will bulge and pop up. An example of this kind of planned shaping can be seen in my Della Robbia Wreath (see color photo on page 38 and detail below). The nuts, fruit, and cones were appliquéd to the background, then stitched around and around to form three-dimensional bloops. To see how this works, cut some

Detail of Della Robbia Wreath.

shapes of different colors and stitch them to a base fabric. Next stitch around the shape until it forms a bloop. If you use a lightweight base fabric, it will bulge more easily with fewer stitches than on a heavier fabric. Notice how much this blooping changes the shape and the size of the base fabric—the higher the bloop, the more the distortion.

There is another way to shape the fabric. If you zig back and forth a lot, as you might for drawing grass, the fabric will gather, grumple, and pucker. Isn't that fun? You can actually sculpt and distort the fabric quite significantly just with the stitches.

Of course if you do not want your fabric all grumpled and blooped you will need to keep it stretched tight while you are stitching. You can use fewer back-and-forth and round-and-round stitches but that may not solve everything. Your hand pressure, holding the fabric straight and stretched while you sew, can make a difference. Try stitches with and without the pressure and stretching and see what happens.

## Other Ways To Change Shape and Texture

The fabric you are working with—both base fabric and applied fabric—is a big factor in the amount of distortion. The heavier, stiffer "learning" base fabric distorts much less than a soft, drapable, thin fabric. Try a variety of base fabrics and also a variety of applied fabrics and see what effects you get with different ones. When sewing down a circle of a soft knit fabric, it is difficult to sew all around it without getting puckers and pleats. That result leads to another thought: Cut a roundish shape of soft fabric. Sew part way around it then stuff the shape with fiberfil and complete the stitching around. Now you have a wonderful raised shape to finish and detail. Think of some other ways you can change the shape and texture of the applied pieces. Maybe tuck them or pleat them as you sew them down. Isn't this exciting? You are free to do whatever you want with the fabric pieces and create all sorts of wonderful effects.

CHAPTER 4

# Materials and Methods

## Attaching and Stabilizing Fabrics

During the process of experimenting and learning, you have been playing with shapes, stitches, actions, and reactions. Placement of the pieces has not been critical. When you become more comfortable with the method and begin to more carefully pre-design your fabric creations you will probably want to find a way to keep the fabric pieces in place until you can get to the sewing machine to sew them down. I find that I often change my mind during the sewing down process, and I will want to move the pieces around. If they are too securely attached, this becomes difficult. For larger patches and ones I may shift, straight pins work well, or sometimes I will use fabric glue sticks. With a bazzillion tiny patches, these temporary glues can be exasperating when the pieces flip off and get lost. Too many straight pins can cause punctured bleeding fingers.

Iron-on (fusible) laminates can be helpful in dealing with small patches. If you iron lightly or touch a few spots on the appliqué with the tip of the iron, they can often be pulled free and repositioned if you want them moved. Fusible laminates come in two major styles. One is a fine web of meltable material that you cut the same size as the appliqué piece, placing the web between the piece and the base fabric, and then ironing to fuse them together. The other variety is a fusible web on paper backing. You can iron this type onto your fabric patch, then cut out the shape, peel off the backing and fuse the patch to the base fabric. An advantage of the paper-backed kind is that you can trace the pattern of your appliqué piece onto the paper backing, then iron the fuse material with the pattern to your appliqué fabric. And, as before, cut out the shape, peel off the paper and fuse to

the base fabric. Be sure to remember to reverse the design so that the bonding web ends up on the back of your cut-out shape.

Both styles of laminate bonding materials are available in a variety of weights, stiffness, and holding powers. The heavier weights tend to stiffen the fabric considerably and some can change the appearance and color. It is always wise to try any of these products on scrap pieces of fabric first to see if the final effect will be what you want. Both bonding types are available in yardage and in ribbon form of various widths.

## Base Fabrics

The piece of fabric I refer to as the base fabric is the one that everything gets attached to. Until now you have been using a fabric with a lot of body for this. Once you have a grasp of the method, you can use almost anything you want. If the fabric you have fallen in love with is lightweight and flimsy, there are ways to make it easier to work on. To reduce stretching and distortion, you will probably want to stiffen or stabilize it. There are many materials and methods available for this—some temporary, some permanent. Paper (non-woven) tear-away materials and wash-away products

can be placed under or over the whole piece or just the design areas and then removed when the stitching is completed. Starches and other water-based stiffeners can be sprayed or brushed onto the fabric, or the fabric may be dipped and dried to stiffen it. These can then be washed out when you are ready, or left in if you want a stiffer product. When choosing a method, be aware of the size of your sewing machine arm and the space you have to maneuver your artwork under the needle. That dimension will be a factor in deciding how stiff and how large a piece you can handle.

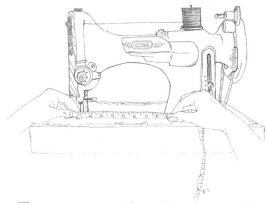

There are many weights and many types of iron-on backings and interfacings that can be successful permanent stiffeners. These are available in knit, woven, and non-woven materials. They are designed for many fabric types from fine sheers to window shade fabrics. Also available are the heat-bonding laminates mentioned earlier that would allow you to bond the chosen fabric to a heavier fabric for stability. Another way to make a softer fabric more usable is to simply baste it to a heavier fabric. The stitches used when you create your design will hold the two pieces together.

Each time I start a new soft picture, it is a whole new adventure. Every group of fabrics requires individual treatment, and new products are constantly appearing for me to try. Part of the excitement is finding the ones that are the most fun to use for each task. Don't be afraid to try different things—the only magic formula is whatever combination works best for you.

## Appliqué Fabrics

The pieces of fabric that you use to create your design can be even more varied than the base fabric. In fact, you can use anything that your machine will stitch on or over. This might include ribbons, yarn, cord, leather, fur, plastic pieces, netting, lace, feathers, grasses—the list goes on and on. The only limitation you have is determined by how you plan to use your creation after it is finished.

Some fabrics and materials can be difficult to sew on. Try a variety of types, weights, and textures so that you and your machine can come to an agreement. Some machines will balk at sewing on certain fabrics.

My machine totally refuses to sew through those lovely suede-look fabrics. This caused some heated discussions. I love the texture, crisp edge, and wonderful colors, but I finally compromised and found substitutes that worked, so my machine and I are friends again.

With some fabrics such as small print calicoes and deep piles, the single drawn line for detailing will tend to visually disappear. Plain, flat-surfaced fabrics show the line drawings more readily. Something that is fun to try with pile fabrics is to flatten the pile with a lot of fill-in stitches in some areas—it gives a high-low look that is very different. Sometimes you may have a problem with looped pile and long-haired fur fabrics. On these, the open or U-shaped foot can get really hung up. Try a variety of types so you can decide if it's worth the hassle.

When the pieces you are cutting out to use for appliqué are small and/or of a loosely woven fabric, the needle action when you sew them down may disintegrate the edges. Iron-on backing or fusible bonding materials work well to minimize this problem. If you don't want to adhere the piece firmly to the base fabric, use an interfacing to stabilize the edges. These are available in many weights and colors and weaves to suit all fabrics.

There are times when you might want the frazzled edges to happen. I fringed some white satin to create a look of feathers on the bird nest in Spring Song (see photo on page 44). On another picture, I sewed down white cotton $1/8$" from the edge and frayed it to look like sea foam (see photo of Shore Birds on page 46). In many of Karen Hagen's quilts, she effectively uses green print fabrics cut and frayed to create leaf edges and evergreen trees (see photo of Mt. Shuksan-Shalom on page 45). She may cut the shapes and pre-wash them to encourage the edges to fray, or, when the fabric frays easily, she will attach the leaf with a single line of machine stitching that forms the leaf vein. These fabric pieces will then fray more and more as the quilt is handled. I'm sure you will discover many more great uses for frayed fabrics in your creative compositions.

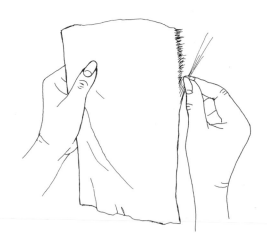

When you are choosing fabrics, remember to carefully consider the use the creation will receive and pick suitable fibers and textures. If wear and washability are not a concern, you can let your imagination soar. There are so many wonderful kinds of fabrics to choose from—cottons, silks and silk looks, rayons, wools and wool looks, corduroys, velvets, metallics—the list goes on and on. Expand your thinking beyond cottons and calicoes, and you will discover a whole new world of possibilities.

## About Thread

Thread is a very important component of free-motion straight-stitch embroidery. The thread, besides holding all of the parts together, creates details, highlights, shadows, and texture. There are many wonderful varieties of thread, both old and new, and in this machine drawing style, anything goes. I use regular sewing thread for both attaching and detailing most of my pictures, but I often add some rayons and metallics for color and excitement. For detailing and drawing, my favorite is black sewing thread, but that is strictly personal preference. This creative method is a wonderful way to use up all those bits and pieces of miscellaneous threads you have been saving. (My cat has a toy box brimming with empty spools in all types and sizes, and it just keeps growing.)

It is a good plan to consider the ultimate use of your artwork when you are choosing thread. It would not be too wise to use antique threads on something that will be worn and laundered often. Some of the older threads break easily and may not be worth the trouble. I have a stash of lovely antique silk threads in gorgeous, time-mellowed colors, that I occasionally use for special effects. Most of the time though, I just enjoy them for their visual effect—arranged on a shelf with the wooden spool edges outlining a softly glowing rainbow of color. (Is that a compulsive collector's justification—or what?) I love to use the new rayon threads for their clear singing colors and shine and the metallic threads for their glitz and shimmer.

The size of the threads will be determined by what your machine will accommodate and also the effect you want. I personally find that the superfine machine embroidery threads tend to disappear too much into the fabric for my style of detailing and drawing. They are great for a smooth satin look if you use a lot of filling stitches. I sometimes use buttonhole twist or topstitching weights for special accent and emphasis. If you try a variety of weights and types, you will soon discover which ones your machine will accept or reject.

One secret to hassle-free thread use is to match your needle to the thread size and type. Some threads have a tendency to heat up and break more readily due to friction as they go through the needle's eye.

Metallic threads are known for breaking easily and will work better if you use a larger needle-eye size. Because they are more fragile, a slower speed and gentle treatment will give the best results. There is a really exciting variety of needle styles with special features for different uses, and more are being developed all the time. Ask your sewing machine supply store to show you the newest ones for your machine.

Some machines will accept the larger, thicker threads gracefully, while others do not. Some machines will only accept the larger threads if they are wound on the bobbin. Threads too bulky to go through a needle's eye can be bobbin-wound also. The bobbin tension will likely need to be adjusted. When the decorative thread is coming from the bobbin, it will be deposited on the underside of the fabric (bobbin side) as you sew. To sew the threads on the face of the artwork, turn it upside down as you sew. This is not a problem, really, just a different approach. It is well worth trying a variety of threads and learning what your sewing machine can do. The effects you get can be really exciting.

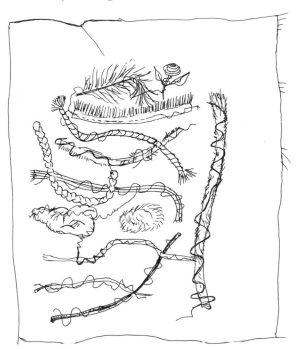

If your machine won't accept the heavier threads, you can couch them on. This involves laying the large thread on the surface of the fabric and stitching back and forth over it with regular thread. (See the illustration above.) Ribbons, yarn, string, cord, and other unusual materials can be added using this method. In Cathy's Robin (see photo on page 44), the real feathers lining the nest were sewn on (couched) using squiggly stitched lines.

Consider the color of the thread as another design variable. I like to use a color that matches or blends with the applied fabric piece to secure it to the

backing fabric. When wear is a consideration, you can use lots of stitches and secure them well without the stitches being obtrusive. (Then, when you add the detail with the contrasting colored thread, the line can be free and creative.) I usually use the same color thread for the top and the bobbin. If the thread tension is balanced, you will see only the surface thread but moving quickly might make the bobbin thread peek through. Some interesting effects can happen if you use two thread colors and purposely adjust the tension to pull the bobbin thread to loop on the surface.

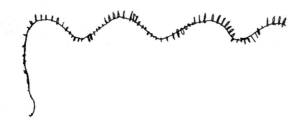

Clear transparent threads are available and can be useful for tacking down the appliqué pieces. This would eliminate the need to change thread color for each different colored piece. Some clear threads are stiffer than others. Some of the transparent threads may melt when a hot iron is used, so check the product and make sure it will work for the use it will receive.

Different colors of threads can be used effectively to create highlights, shadow, small color dots, color-blended accents, squiggly lines, and much more. Try using a thread the color of the background fabric when adding your appliqué. This will soften the edges and blend it to the background. If you are making a furry critter use the critter color to draw the fur out beyond the cut shape. Then use thread in lighter and darker tones to create highlights and shadows.

Grasses and wheat and fence-row weeds and shrubs can all be made using a variety of thread colors. For an illusion of distance, start with the lighter colors and draw ziggles and zags over each other. Continue layering with increasingly darker colors. For Jane's Winter View (see photo on page 37), I made the dried grasses against the snow starting with off-white thread, then browns, and ending with rust.

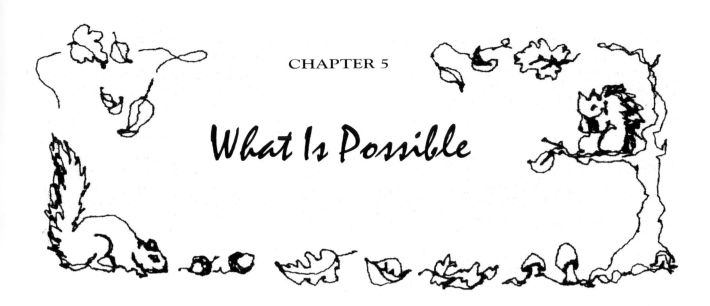

**CHAPTER 5**

# What Is Possible

## Not Just For Pictures

Although most of the illustrations in this book are of the soft pictures that I make, there are no limits to the kinds of fabric items that free-motion straight stitch will enhance. I usually suggest a picture as a first project. The reason is that for a picture you do not have to be as concerned with wear and washability and therefore you cut down on the list of "think-abouts." You can go through the learning process with more design freedom, and when you are comfortable with the process, you can more easily include items that require restrictions and careful planning. Here is a list of some possible uses for fabrics enriched with free-motion straight-stitch embroidery. You can, I am sure, think of others.

Pictures and wall hangings

Clothing and accessories (bags, scarves, belts, jewelry)

Quilts, coverlets, bedding, table linens, bath linens

Curtains and draperies, upholstery, slipcovers, pillows

Toys, dolls, games, critters

Three-dimensional soft sculpture

Books, cards, announcements, awards

## Choose Materials and Methods To Suit the Use

If you are creating items that will need to be laundered or dry cleaned, and items that will be subjected to wear, care must be taken when choosing fabrics and threads. Think carefully also about the placement of the design, how much stitching you will use, and how well you will attach the appliqué pieces. For all household fabric items, there are many kinds of stress and wear involved. When laundering, using fibers that react similarly should be planned, and pre-shrinking the fabrics is important. For some uses, you should consider the potential for the sun to fade and deteriorate the fabrics and threads.

While planning the designs for different uses, keep in mind the distortion that occurs. Fabrics with heavy layers of stitching and multiple-layered fabrics may be more prone to distortion and may be inappropriate for some uses. Lumps, bumps, grumples, and bloops could be quite uncomfortable to sit on—whether on the seat of a chair or the rear side of clothing. A little careful pre-thought can save you much grief at a later time.

When you stitch over and through layers of fabric, there is always some distortion and shrinkage. That is one of the effects that gives this art method its unique charm. You just need be aware that it will happen. The time to plan for distortion is in the early design stage. When making a soft picture, I always allow a minimum of three inches extra fabric on each edge. For example, if I want an 18" x 24" finished picture, I cut out the base fabric at 24" x 30". When all the stitching is completed, I can trim the edges and square the corners again without having to cut away some of the picture. When making quilt blocks using free-motion stitching, be sure to allow adequate extra fabric. Nothing is more exasperating than having a quilt block come out too small. For clothing that you are making and want to free-stitch design, it is wise not to cut the pattern pieces from the fabric until after you have free-stitched the design on it. Draw the outline of the clothing pattern piece on the fabric, allowing extra space around it. Free-stitch your design, then re-mark the pattern piece and cut it out. If you are working on an already constructed garment, use precautions to minimize the distortion.

There is another way to create designs with lots of fabric layers and stitches without distorting the base fabric. You can make a separate "patch" of the design and then sew the patch onto the base fabric. Start with a muslin or organdy, do all of your layering and stitching, cut away the excess muslin or organdy, and sew this design to your garment or picture. When sewing the patch on, you will need only enough stitches to secure it and blend it to the background,

and any bloops or grumples are on the patch only. The patch method was used on the cover's machine-stitched picture to add the cat and the sewing machine. Other examples include the birds in Cathy's Robin (see photo on page 44) and Our Feathered Friend (see photo on page 47).

Many of my soft pictures consist of several "levels." I will make a background or outdoor scene, add a window and wall, then place objects in front of the window. Each step is completed before I start the next level. I will often use the "patch" method for objects in the foreground that I want to detail heavily, such as the cat and bird in "Cat Nap" (see photo below).

Cat Nap, made by the author.

There is another reason for pre-detailing some shapes added to a picture. When stitching over a fabric, the stitches draw the fabric tight against the background, sometimes causing creases and wrinkles. You may not want that. For example, if you want to appliqué an apple onto the picture, you could stitch it around the outside, and it would look nice and round and smooth. If you then decide to add a stem or blossom end and some stitches for shadows and highlights, the result would be a lumpy, wrinkled apple. If, instead, the apple is detailed (adding shadows, highlights, and so forth) before sewing it down onto the picture, it will stay nice and round and smooth because the stitching to the background is only around the outside edges. The apples in A is for Apple (see color photo on page 39) were detailed, then added to the picture.

Separately Detailed Apples Ready to Use In A Is For Apple

## Quilting

Are you aware, or have you noticed that free-motion straight stitch is what you use for hand-guided machine quilting? There are many wonderful books written about machine quilting so here I will only discuss a few experiences I have encountered as it relates to free-motion straight-stitch designing.

Free-stitch machine designs can be considered complete, or you may want to add a filler and a backing and make a quilt "sandwich." Stitching through all of these layers (quilting) holds everything together so it won't be as likely to sag or shift. When you are making a picture to hang on the wall, you may decide to stretch it and frame it, or make a soft picture—your choice. Soft pictures, especially larger ones, usually will be more satisfactory if they are layered and quilted. They tend to hang and lie flat better.

The decision to be made is whether you want to have the quilting stitches be an important part of your finished design or supplement and echo the design lines. I usually complete my picture, layer it, and then decide where quilting lines will enhance the design. In "March Winds, April Showers" (see photo on page 40), I used the quilting stitches to create grass texture, rain streaks, and cloud delineation

If you are making a quilt block or quilt top, keep in mind that a lot of fabric layers and gobs of stitches create very stiff areas that are difficult to quilt through by hand. Quilting these areas by machine is more feasible, but outlining and stitch-in-the-ditch may

work better. Expand your thinking about what this free-wheeling stitched line can do for you. Not only does it give a line-drawn quality to your artwork, but it can create negative line or accent on the spaces between the lines when you quilt. If you want something to jump forward, quilt around it.

While on the subject of quilting and quiltmaking, I should mention that free-motion straight-stitch drawing could be a really fun way to enhance and embellish (see Carol Olsen's Chaotic Cosmos with gold metallic-thread used for the quilting lines in the photo on page 42). Sometimes, you can even rescue pieced work that needs some pizzazz.

## Enhancing Fabrics

Changing Polka Dots to Flowers

Many ordinary fabrics can easily become very special and exciting by stitching over the fabric print to create something new. Polka dots, for example, with free-motion straight stitch, could turn into flowers or balloons or fat little fish. Vague shapes or blocks of color with line-drawn details can become buildings or craggy rocks or windows. A fabric printed with amorphous colored shapes can become a cluster of birds, a herd of elephants, a gaggle of geese. Add birds

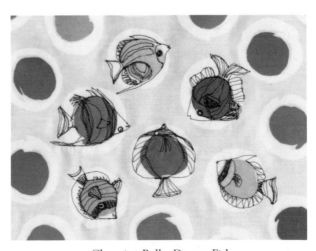

Changing Polka Dots to Fish

Detailing Flower-Patterned Fabric

or airplanes or hot air balloons to cloud fabrics. Make seascapes from swirling prints, seashores from sandy speckled prints; add insects and flowers to grassy and leafy prints. Let your imagination run— decide what is hiding there and lure it out. Use that powerful machine-drawn line to define, re-design, and create new images. An ordinary print fabric can come alive if you add accents of bright rayon or silk threads or metallic threads.

Creating Birds From Amorphous Shapes

Those of you who collect or create hand-dyed or hand-painted fabrics have a wonderful source of fabrics to enhance with stitchery. Many times with dyed fabrics, a vague "sort-of-looks-like" pattern emerges. You can use your new line drawing method to bring your design into focus. Perhaps that batik or hand-painted piece didn't quite turn out as you wanted it. Try some touch-up with stitches or added fabric pieces or both. You could be started on a whole new design direction.

## Cut Out and Rebuild

Here is another way to rework printed fabrics. You can cut the motifs from a print and reassemble them on a new background and add free-stitch details. Find several different wonderful fish prints and create a tropical fish scene with fish cut from more than one print. Assemble them on a water-look background and add plants and shells and snails. Collect wild animal or dinosaur prints and make a jungle scene. The method is simple. Create the background, then cut the critters out around the outline and sew them to the

background. Detail the pieces with free-motion straight stitch, using the printed lines as a guide.

Flowers, bees, and butterflies are great to mix and combine using a variety of fabrics. Choose flowers that go well together in color and proportion. I like to call these flower collections my own version of *broderie perse*. During the 18th century in America, the popular printed chintz fabrics were not readily available. Wanting to have bedcoverings in the then current style, our ingenious ancestors devised a way to make the coveted fabrics go much farther. They cut out the flowers and motifs from the chintz and appliquéd them to a more available plain-colored fabric. They often rearranged the flowers in new clusters to create balanced designs. Because it re-sembled Persian embroidery, the technique became known as *broderie perse*. The pieces were hand-applied with turned-under raw edges. Today I trim the flowers right to the outline and use straight stitch to sew them down and detail them. Doesn't this sound like a great way to use a special fabric and create your own personal design? My own version of *broderie perse* can be seen on the back of my tunic "Roses" (see photo).

Rose Tunic With *Broderie Perse* Panel

## Lace

I could not possibly discuss fabric pictures and free-motion straight stitch without talking about lace. For years I have been enamored with lace—it is an exquisite art form. Because I have collected and studied lace for a long time, I like to use pieces of it in my soft pictures. Usually I will use bits and pieces of an antique lace that is too tattered and torn for usefulness otherwise and that has no historical or sentimental significance. Using these in my pictures allows me to prolong my enjoyment of a beautiful lace. I have made several "bouquets" of lace flower motifs snipped from a variety of contemporary and old lace pieces. Flowers seem to be a common theme in lacemaking.

Lace Bouquet, made by the author.

To make a lace bouquet, cut carefully around the flower shapes. Often this involves snipping connecting bars or threads. Arrange the flowers on a black or dark-colored background fabric. Lace leaves can be found or they can be created from flower petals or a sheer fabric. Flower stems can be sewn in or made of narrow ribbon or cord. I like to combine white and cream and ecru motifs in one bouquet to add variation. Pin in place and then in free-motion mode, sew everything down using straight stitch or a loose zigzag stitch. The stitches should hold the pieces in place with a light airy touch. Wiggly sewing lines are usually better then straight. Add details such as sprays of tiny flowers, stems, and extra leaves using free stitch.

Not only can you use lace in making your art pieces, but beautiful lace can be made with free-motion straight stitch on net. I have always been intrigued with lace called "needle-run." When machine-made nets that didn't run were first developed in 1808, they became the basis for several new types of handmade lace such as tambour, lace appliqué, and needle-run. These became an important part of the Irish lace industry that developed during the potato famine of the 1800s. Although originally made using a hand needle or hook with embroidery threads, these methods are easily adaptable to hand-guided machine stitching methods. Traditionally,

Victoria's Bouquet, made by the author

needle-run used two weights of thread—a heavier one to outline the shapes, and finer threads to fill the spaces. The filling stitches were formed by working over and under the mesh hexagons in several different patterns. To recreate needle-run using machine-free straight stitch, you will want to keep the net stretched tight. Make the outline of the shapes (flowers or leaves for example) using heavier thread like buttonhole twist, then fill in with stitches formed with fine sewing thread. The "filling" stitches can be ziggles or squiggles or cross hatches or spirals (see samples on page 14, the Doodle Page).

Contemporary Needle-Run Table Topper and Three Net-Appliqué Handkerchiefs

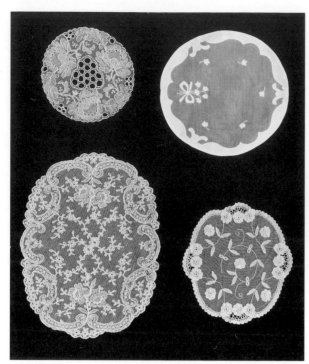

Traditional Needle-Run and Net-Appliqué

Appliquéd net was traditionally made by laying organdy or fine muslin over the net and then outlining the shapes with heavy thread. In some areas they would cut away the fabric and net and then fill these open spaces with needle lace stitches. Needle-run embroidery was used to form stems and leaf veins. You can adapt the same process using free-motion machine embroidery, and you will have beautiful lace, designed by you.

## Layering Sheer Fabrics

I have always loved color—not just bright singing colors, but how colors interact and blend and create moods and feelings. When I started to use a variety of fabrics to create different effects, I soon discovered the magic and excitement of working with sheer fabrics in a rainbow of colors. I found I could produce a "watercolor" effect using overlapping sheers, blending the colors together to create a new color. Sheer fabrics in pale colors and in white are great for diffusing and blending and creating a soft, foggy look. You can use dark-colored sheers to make wonderful shadows. Some of the sheer fabrics have a shimmer or sheen that can add exciting highlights to your artwork. Mary Goodson of Eugene, Oregon, "paints" beautiful scenes using sheer fabrics and hand embroidery stitches, layer upon layer. Her pictures have an amazing depth. From Mary I learned that if you use a bright-white base fabric and layer bright-colored sheers over that, you will have clear singing colors.

All see-through fabrics work well for blending, and different textures create different effects. Some of the sheer fabrics I use are nets (in a variety of mesh sizes), organdy, chiffon, silk organza, nylon stockings, sheer knits, and curtain sheers. To find sheers I look in stores that supply bridal and formal fabrics, drapery fabrics, and craft supplies. The very fine net called illusion veiling is available in a variety of colors and white and black. In the store on the bolt, you see many layers and it will look bright-colored. A single layer can be almost invisible, so it may take several layers to create the intensity of color you want. To get a feel for color layering, collect a variety of net, knit, and woven sheer fabrics in several colors. Cut a base fabric of white cotton about 12" x 12". Cut strips and pieces of the sheer fabrics and layer them onto the base fabric. Keep overlapping and piling them on. Notice how the colors will visually mix and create another color. Red and blue become purple; yellow and blue turn green; yellow and red turn orange where they overlap. Keep adding different colored pieces until the colors become muddy and loose their zing. Then pull some back off and overlap different colors. It is a great way to play with color.

When I made my picture "Spring Song" (see photo on page 44), I was playing with shapes and colors with no scene in mind. When I added a piece of dark brown organza it made me think of a tree branch against a sunset sky. So I developed the idea of a nest, eggs, and the robin, still using sheer pieces of color. The drawing and detailing with black thread brought the soft diffused shapes into focus and gave the picture its definition.

The picture "Tropical Fish Wish" (see photo on page 48) was made using a lot of sheer fabrics. First I created the cat's face on the base fabric, complete with whiskers, fur, and pink tongue. Then I layered sheer fabric over the cat in bands and streaks of colors, tucking in fish and water plants at various levels. I wanted the cat's face to be way in the background—something you slowly became aware of, so I kept layering. Suddenly, I thought, "I've gone too far and lost my cat!" But when I stood back away from the work, I realized he was still there, peering through the fish tank. That is when I stopped layering. There is no formula for designing with sheer fabrics—you just add, subtract, and add again until it looks right to you.

Sheers are wonderful to use for creating an illusion of translucency, transparency, and motion. Consider using sheer fabrics for bees or hummingbird wings in flight, for clear glass jars, windows, curtains blowing in the breeze, soft floating feathers, water flowing or clear jelly in a glass. I know you can think of many more ideas.

For highlights or a glint of sunshine, white or yellow sheers work well. Shadows are easy to create using darker-toned sheers. A shadow shape can be added on top, and the color, texture, and pattern of the shaded fabric still shows through.

When working with small pieces of sheer fabrics, you will find that they are easy to lose. Some crisp fabrics like net and organdy will attach themselves to any fabric that comes close. If you have a fuzzy sweater on and reach over the layered artwork to add another piece, suddenly the artwork will be bare and you will be wearing an array of blended colors. To minimize the problem, I generally pin the pieces down with straight pins as I go. Remember to remove the pins from each layer as you add the next or the pins might become buried so deeply they won't be retrievable. When satisfied with the effect, I cover the whole picture with a single piece of fine white illusion veiling. One layer will be almost invisible and will hold everything in place while it is sewn down.

I like to use a thread color that blends with the colors and sew lines from side to side or top to bottom to secure the sheers. Smoothly flowing lines of stitching that somewhat follow the edges of the major color pieces work best. If you plan to use your new color-blended piece as a background for a lot of stitch drawing and appliqué, fewer tack-down lines are needed.

## Written Words

I know you tried writing your name in the doodle exercise in Chapter 2. I hope you had fun with it and will try writing many things with this new drawing tool. Writing is a great way to practice the method and to learn to control the line direction. The "continuous line" quality makes script writing much easier than doing individual letters. (See more information on page 14, the Doodle Page.)

My personal feeling is that it is very important for all artists who create an original design to sign

Detail from Pretty Maids Quilt

their artwork. What better way for fabric artists to sign their creations than writing with thread? Also important for those of us who work with fabric is to sign, date, and give pertinent information on a label attached to each piece of fabric art produced. Your descendants will thank you—really! The labels I put on the back of my soft pictures include the following information: my name, year made, and any other gems of information such as for whom made, awards won, and for what occasion, if any. With all of this information documented there will never be a question of originator. We, as fabric artists, need to stand tall and proud—even with our early creations. They represent our best at the time of making and come from the heart—a unique expression of ourselves.

Stitches and thread are more permanent than most inks for writing, and once you have practiced a while, it is a quick and easy way to personalize your work. Using machine writing, you can put your name on all of your clothes with a discrete inside label. For a very personal fashion statement, use your name as an embellishment. No design is more uniquely you than a stylized version of your own name. With this new skill you can use the written word as a design element to enhance quilts, clothing, and wall pieces.

Machine writing is a wonderful way to document occasions and happenings and family history. My quilt called "Pretty Maids" (details shown on this page) began as a stamped "kit" from the early 1920s that I found in my mother's trunk. My grandmother had sent it to her to be made for me as a baby quilt. The package consisted of "stamped" blocks and pieces of print fabrics ready to cut out, appliqué and embroider. My mother embroidered two blocks, and then it was put away to finish later. (Sound familiar?) When I found it, I decided I would finish it for my first

Free-Motion Writing on Pretty Maids Quilt

granddaughter, so I carefully followed directions for the hand embroidery and appliqué. I looked at it then and decided "this is my gift and creation and I want to honor the four generations of women in my family." I used my machine writing skills to make four blocks that gave the maiden names, married names, and living dates of each woman. I added a hand-appliquéd ribbon to tie the generations together. Now my granddaughter has a lovely personal family document that will last for future generations to enjoy.

To design the writing, try several styles and arrangements first with pencil on paper. Then practice your writing with the sewing machine on a stiff base fabric until you feel comfortable with the results. Remember that this is a brand new tool, and the control comes only with practice. It is like learning to write with the pencil grasped in your toes! Usually you will find that you will develop a whole new writing style—quite different from your hand-held pen or pencil style. You will feel very awkward at first, but if you allow yourself some time, you will be creating your own unique writing with accomplished ease very soon.

Cut the base fabric for your written message with plenty of extra fabric so you can center and trim

it later and not "run off the page." Stabilize the fabric: This is one place where you will not want grumples and bloops. To help you center the writing and come out reasonably straight, use a removable marker to mark a vertical center line and a line for each row of writing on the fabric. Next, with your paper and pencil version beside you, write your message.

Secure the threads at the beginning and end of each word and trail the threads to the next word. When dotting an "i," I recommend that you complete the word and then go back to make the dot. Make a small circle of stitches centered above the "i" and then fill it in. Trail the threads to the next word, and clip off close to the fabric after the writing is completed. To cross a "t," follow the diagrams at the bottom of this page as you make the letter: Stitch upward to the top of the "t," then down to the cross point, to the right, back to the cross point, to the left, and then back to the cross point to continue downward while completing the letter.

When you have completed the writing, clip off all trailing threads close to the fabric. You can now center the message by marking and trimming off excess fabric. Hand-appliqué your message on the back of your artwork.

## Translating Children's Art

How many times as a parent or grandparent were you presented with a wonderful "artwork" created lovingly by a child? Mine were usually taped to the refrigerator, then finally discarded when worn and torn. Some of these drawings are such gems and hold so much love and spontaneity that it is difficult to part with them. When my children were little, I felt I had to capture that love, and thus I began a creative direction that has given me worlds of pleasure and satisfaction through the years. Using free-motion straight stitch, I "translated" the children's pictures onto fabric. This is such an easy thing to do and can give so much pleasure to both child and adult, I urge you to try it. The secret of success is to recreate the drawing as exactly as you can so you retain that happy unrestrained freedom of the child's artwork.

In 1970 I branched out and began to recreate children's drawings at fairs and quilt shows. After all of these years, I am surprised by how much I still enjoy the experience. At some large fairs I have translated as many as 40 drawings in one session, and the time just flies by. It is a really wonderful way to interact with a child one on one. When you are recreating a child's drawing, the two of you are totally focused. Children will open up and tell you about the drawings—what they represent—and wonderful expanded stories about

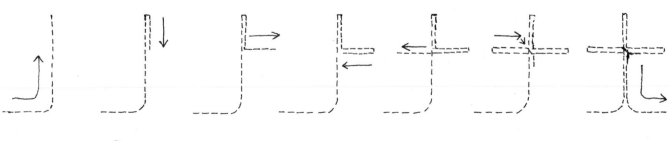

the subject and themselves. Often they will re-choose some of the colors and want some things added or left out. If you spend a little time letting them choose the fabrics you use to recreate their crayon colors and involve them in the process, you both will gain so much. Try to work with one child at a time and be careful that a more dominant child is not there to

interfere with the personal interaction.

The process is simple. Have the child draw a picture on paper with crayons or pencil. Cut a base fabric piece the size of the drawing. Cut out fabric pieces the size and shape of the objects in the child's drawing. With black thread, sew the color pieces down and then detail them. Use the thread to draw in features and line drawn details (grass, birds, faces). I like to have the child put his or her name on the paper drawing, and I copy the signature as closely as possible. If the child wants me to, I will add his or her age. When the picture is complete, we make a trade—the child gets the fabric rendition, and I get the paper drawing.

The pride and delight shown in happy faces when children are given their fabric art is worth every moment you spend and more! If you decide you want to use these artworks in a quilt or to sew onto clothing or to be framed, be sure to allow extra fabric around the piece

for seams. Children tend to use the whole piece of paper when they draw so you need to cut your base fabric larger and then you will be able to duplicate the drawing exactly to size.

When I first started to work with my own children and to translate their art, I thought that I should tidy it up and change it to my version of what they intended. This was a BIG mistake! This destroyed the freshness and the freedom of their work. My youngest son brought home a wonderful butterfly drawing from school one day. It was a big orange butterfly with many wonderful shapes drawn into the wings with crayons. He had carefully cut out all around both the butterfly and his name. It was an inspiring design so I decided to make a large wall hanging using his design idea. As we worked together

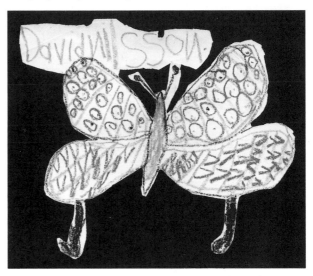

David's Butterfly, A paper drawing made by the author's son.

planning the piece and discussing the fabrics and colors, I explained how I would use several of the butterfly colors together in strips to make the frame around the butterfly. David was outraged. "Mommy," he said "I cut the butterfly out so it could fly!" We did not frame it.

The flying butterfly is a lesson I have not forgotten. One of the joys of interacting with children is being able to listen carefully and hear what they are feeling. If you are relaxed and can enjoy the interchange and that moment in time, it becomes a wonderful loving gift for both you and the child.

Remember when working with children's art, the secret of success is to recreate the picture as the child drew it. See the picture as he or she has visualized it and be sure to retain that wonderful freshness and joy.

I'm sure that all parents have heard the preschool and summer-holiday lament, "There's nothing to do." I discovered a great way to chase away the blues for both child and parent. Try making pictures together using machine free-motion straight stitchery. This activity will develop your own confidence and give you some great one-on-one time with your child.

First, collect "scrap bag" fabric pieces and a sturdy base fabric and prepare your machine for free-motion sewing. Next, with your child close by, ask, "What shall we draw?" The adventure begins. Together, choose fabrics to add to the picture. Let it grow into a wonderful *shared* creation. Maybe your theme could be a jungle scene with all kinds of amazing critters coming from the scrap bag to live in your and your child's picture. This spontaneous designing not only affords you some special shared moments with your child, but also encourages the child to think creatively. Designing this way does not allow you to be precise and uptight. Instead, it promotes free and unself-conscious creation. You are free to say, "This piece sort of looks like an elephant. Shall we put it over here?" and then have a good giggle together because it turns out to be a three-legged purple elephant standing on a flower!

Children, as they develop dexterity, can use the sewing machine themselves to create their own fabric pictures. This is a wonderful way to introduce them to the fun and excitement of using this handy tool. Gone are all of those deadly uptight notions about following the line exactly. Instead, they are free to experiment and get acquainted with the parts and action of the sewing machine. Children pick up very quickly on the idea of using the stitches to draw lines and to create wonderful shapes and squiggles.

When he was a 6-year-old, my son David created a fabulous flower garden using the sewing machine in

Chris's Cat, made by the author from her son's paper drawing.

free-motion mode (see the photo on page 34). For the background, he chose a piece of blue-and-white fabric he had tie-dyed. It made a great sky. He then delved into the scrap bag for his fabrics. His choices for flowers were very innovative: He passed by the floral prints and, instead, cut various flower shapes from a yellow shell, a cluster of two-toned polka dots, a piece from a paisley print, a geometric print, and some plain fabrics. He made a piece of green velvet into a fuzzy caterpillar. He backed a piece cut from lace with red and yellow for butterfly wings. He picked a yellow satin for the sun and gave it a big orange thread smile and zigzag rays. He did no pre-drawing. Instead, he designed directly on the base fabric as he found the fabric pieces that he wanted to add.

This is a wonderful method for an adult to use, also. I urge you to try working from the scrap bag to the picture, designing as you go. The freedom, the sense of adventure, and the excitement of discovery are very rewarding. The happiness and delight you experience will inevitably result in a wonderful artistic expression.

**Storytime**, 25" x 28", made by the author.

**In Flight**,
15" x 18",
made by Carole Sheldon
of South Colby,
Washington.

**David's Flower Garden**,
27" x 23",
made by the author's son,
David Nilsson, at age 6.

David Nilsson 6yrs

**Christmas Angel,**
*14" tall,*
made by the author.

**Wynken, Blynken, and Nod,**
*22" x 33",*
made by the author.

**Palouse Hills Quilt**, 64" x 88", designed and free-stitch appliquéd by the author;
borders designed by Vicki Purviance;
quilt hand-appliquéd, assembled, and quilted by the Palouse Patchers of Moscow, Idaho.

**Jane's Winter View**, 35" x 27", made by the author for Dave and Jane Olson of Ames, Iowa.

**Coastal Dreams**, 49" x 40", made by Pattie Brunette of Port Orchard, Washington.

**Della Robbia Wreath,**
15" circle,
made by the author.

**Harvest Jewels,** 24" x 24", made by the author.

**A Is For Apple**, 20" x 30", made by the author.

**March Winds,
April Showers,**
21" x 24",
made by the author.

**Blue Gossamer Wings,**
19" x 22",
made by the author.

**Catch a Falling Star**, 45" x 45", made by the author. A pattern begins on page 70.

**Chaotic Cosmos**,
48" x 41", made by Carol Olsen
of Bainbridge Island, Washington.

**Chaotic Cosmos**, detail showing use
of metallic thread.

**Captain Kirk's Backyard**,
23" X 25",
made by Kendra Allen
of Paulsbo, Washington.

**Chinese Dragon Kimono**, made by the author
and Barbara Wenders of Moscow, Idaho.

**Northern Sunset**,
48" x 48",
made by the author's sister,
Marian Sims of Elko,
British Columbia, Canada.

**Spring Song,**
12" x 12",
made by the author.

**Cathy's Robin,**
27" x 34",
made by the author
for Mark and Cathy Griswold
of Lyons, Oregon.

**Mt. Shuksan-Shalom,**
96" x 86",
made by Karen Schoepflin Hagen
of Genesee, Idaho

**The Edge of Night,**
38" x 45",
made by Karen Schoepflin Hagen
of Genesee, Idaho.

45

**Shore Birds,**
29" x 33",
made by the author
for Charles and Peggy Jackson
of Kensington, California

**Johnny's Dinosaur Quilt,**
45" x 48",
made by Barbara Wenders
of Moscow, Idaho.

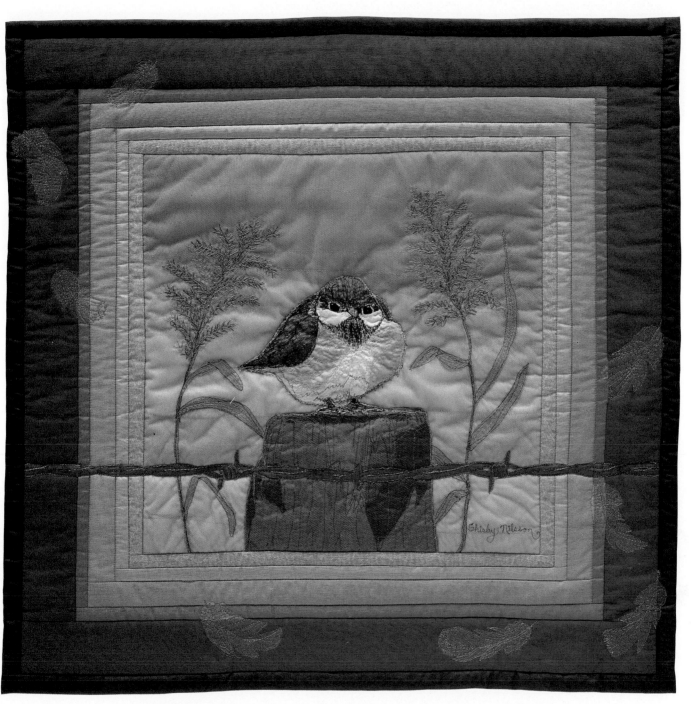

**Our Feathered Friend**, 25" x 25", made by the author from a drawing by her daughter-in-law, Jackie Nilsson. A pattern begins on page 64.

**Tropical Fish Wish**, 33" x 29", made by the author for her son David Nilsson
of Seattle, Washington.

CHAPTER 6

# Designing Free

Apples and Angels and Bumble Bees Buzzing.
Cats and Lace Curtains and Daisies in Dozens.
Birds Eggs and Eventide, Fairies and Feathers.
Gazebos in Gardens and Hares in the Heather.

## Inspiration

One of the questions I am asked most frequently is "Where do you get your ideas?" My answer is "from the heart." Life is so full of wonderful things that I never run out of ideas. When you first set out to create a picture that is all your own, the most important thing is that the subject you choose be dear to your heart. If you love what you are depicting, that love will shine right through. In the beginning stages of learning a new skill, you have many things to experience and coordinate, so adding "learning how to design" may seem like just too much. That is fine—find the process that gives you the most satisfaction. If you see a picture or a design that you really like, and you change it from painted canvas or photo to a fabric composition, you are redesigning by making choices of substitution. When learning a new craft, most of us start out by using someone else's design. As we become more familiar with the method, we begin to develop our own style. Soon ideas will come that we want to depict in our own way. Creating your own design, as scary as it may seem, is very much worth trying. You can spend a lot of time creating a piece of fabric art, and if that art is your own design, the feeling of pride and accomplishment increases immensely.

Incidentally, when you use someone else's design, an important thing to do is always to give credit to the source. When the design is your own, you as the artist are producing a personal expression of how you feel about the subject and how you want the viewer to feel. By being both the designer and creator, you control the whole process. What a mind trip!

## The Design Approach

Take a deep breath and take that first step. Say to yourself "I am going to design something!" There, that really feels good, and it is a positive start. The next step is to fill your mind with things you love, or perhaps something you feel strongly about and love to hate. What kinds of images do the thoughts bring to mind? Do you love flower gardens on a summer day? Are the bees buzzing and the butterflies flitting? Are you picturing daisies bathed in summer sunshine? Now you have a picture idea—a great beginning. For the next step you should gather a stack or roll of sketch paper—just scribble-on and throw-away stuff. Begin to put your ideas on paper. Make very rough sketches of what you visualize. If even rough sketches make you too uptight, write down words. Remember that these sketches are just for you to organize your ideas. Do not be critical of yourself or allow anyone else to criticize. This is just the initial think stage. Think about different angles or points of view. How would your garden look to a bird flying over it? Or to a cricket in the grass? Or to a rabbit hopping by? How would the garden look viewed through a window? Whatever ideas pop into your mind draw or write them on the paper, no matter how off-the-wall they may seem. These can all be incorporated or discarded later. This is your fun, open-your-mind dream time. No thought is too outrageous. When you have filled lots of pages and exhausted your ideas, move on to the next stage. Go back over your idea doodles and make some choices.

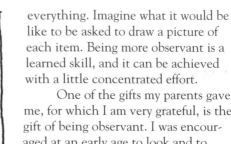

When you are both learning a new skill and experiencing designing your own picture for the first time, a good plan is to keep it simple. The fewer the parts and ideas you incorporate the better. For example, instead of a whole garden you may want to concentrate on one clump of flowers or even a close-up of a single daisy. By using this approach, your first efforts will move along much more quickly. With each picture you finish, your experience will increase and your confidence will build. Once you have chosen an idea and a focus, you can use your original sketches to draw a rough idea of the placement of the parts. The design of your picture begins to emerge.

## Look and See

The next step in creating your own design I call "observation." Every artist and designer is a keen observer. Even those who use abstract images only they can interpret, are successful only if they are very familiar with the subject. We all tend to go through life looking at our world but not really seeing it. Perhaps you have played the game where someone brings a tray of objects and then takes it away, and you are asked to write down what was on the tray. Unless you really concentrate, it is difficult to remember

everything. Imagine what it would be like to be asked to draw a picture of each item. Being more observant is a learned skill, and it can be achieved with a little concentrated effort.

One of the gifts my parents gave me, for which I am very grateful, is the gift of being observant. I was encouraged at an early age to look and to really see the wonderful world we live in. When I was a small child, my sisters and I were directed not just to see the flower or the bird, but to see the rose or to see the robin. Our traveling time was shortened by games of "How many different trees can you name" and "Who will see the first hawk?" Admittedly, life and cars moved much more slowly in those days, but the idea is still valid. You can give the wonderful gift of observation to your children and grandchildren. It is a lifelong gift and they will be forever grateful. All of us, no matter where we are in our life cycle, can learn to observe more keenly and to store the images in our memory banks for future use.

To realize just how unobservant we normally are, try to draw your cat or dog or your child's face without the subject in front of you. Then go and find them and draw while looking carefully. When you duplicate a subject by drawing, you learn to look much more closely and see much more detail. Spend a little time each day examining things closely. We seldom allow ourselves the time to just look and see. When was the last time you allowed yourself to watch a spider weave a web of silken strands? Or watched an ant cut a piece of leaf and carry it across the rough terrain? It takes just minutes, and it is so very worth the time.

Whenever you see something that pleases you, draw or sketch it, with notes to yourself all over it. In

no time you will be looking at your world with a new intensity and excitement. Above all, avoid feelings of "I can't do that." You can try, and in doing so succeed, as each step of learning is a victory. Allow yourself to learn and enjoy the experience. The drawings and sketches that you do are for you alone. They are your aid to becoming more observant. If you want to share your drawings with someone, by all means do, but be sure that you do not allow them to dampen your progress with negative reactions. Once you have some images that you feel good about, create them in fabric. You will feel so accomplished!

An important step in learning to be observant is to first erase all preprogrammed ideas. Preconceived notions of how things look will interfere with the way you see. When we were young children we were told that the sky is blue and trees are green. This is not entirely true. The sky can be many colors. The color changes as you go from morning to night, from spring through winter, from sunlight to overcast. Even a "clear blue" sky is a different color at the horizon or near the sun. Trees have all sorts of colors. Besides the many variations of green, they have new leaves and old dried leaves that might be brown, gold, red or purple. Different colors are reflected in sunshine and shadow and from the top and underside of leaves. Who says we have to follow traditional color ideas anyway? Probably the same people who want us to "stay within the lines." Free yourself to color and draw things as you see them and feel them.

If, in your memory, you always visualized Great Aunt Hepzibah as being very purple—color her purple. This is your visualization, and it can be whatever you want it to be. Design is very personal, and what you like is determined by your own past experiences. You may love the color blue because you had a favorite blue sweater when you were a child. Or you may dislike blue because that nasty kid down the block always wore it. This does not mean that blue is good or bad, but it merely determines your reaction to it. A walk through any museum will illustrate how diverse people's likes and dislikes are. Something that is off balance may make you very uncomfortable but be very stimulating and exciting for someone else. Just as some people prefer quiet and repose, others like action and contrast. The one to say what gives you visual pleasure is you.

## Research and Filing

Once you have listed the things you like and have picked a subject, the next step is research. We seldom are able to have the subject of our picture in front of us for the close observation this step requires. Even if we do, the subject would not likely stay just the same while we make the fabric picture. My cat will mysteriously disappear when I grab a camera or a sketchpad. So instead of relying on her for close observation, I turn to my clipping file. I am a compulsive and aggressive magazine clipper. Whenever I see something that I may use sometime, out come the scissors. (This has created irate family members at times.) The magazine clippings plus greeting cards, calendars, and junk mail all get dropped into file folders. This is a system

that works well for me. I have a file drawer for flora and a drawer for fauna; a drawer for people and a drawer for objects. When I want to include a cat in my picture, I go to the fauna file, pull animals and then cats, domestic. Here I can find that "just right" pose, and my cat doesn't have to get all snarly when I try to pose her just the right way. The clippings I choose go into a new working folder along with the sketched ideas. As I develop the picture in fabric, the reference material is always handy. There are some magazines that I cannot bear to cut up, and also books that have excellent reference material. If a copy machine is an option, I will copy the pages for my files. I also keep a sheet of lined paper in each file folder, and when I find useful ideas in books, I will record the book and page number. I developed this system over many years, and now it saves me much time and searching (and cat bites). Perhaps it will give you some ideas for working out a resource file of your own. This is the way I like to approach design development. You may prefer to use photographs or pictures, draw from memory, or use purely abstracted forms. Be sure to pursue a direction that feels right for you.

## Evaluation

Inspiration is all around us—in nature, in the human environment, in our memory, in history, and in our hearts. Once you understand what can be created using free-motion straight stitch, you will see possibilities everywhere. Just open your mind and feel free to try

whatever you want. Always remember that this is your creation from your heart. If your best friend or aunt doesn't like it, that is all right. How you feel about it is what is important.

Now, if you do not like the creation you just finished, that is another matter. You have several choices. You can use it as padding in the dog's bed, you can give it to a not very favorite relative, you can use it to scrub the walls. (Those stitches make great scrubbers.) Or—and this is my personal favorite—you can use the experience and the product as a learning tool. Never consider anything you make as a failure. Think of all the skill experience you gained when producing the picture and also the feelings of satisfaction and accomplishment.

One of the very best ways to learn and grow is to critically and unemotionally analyze your own work. Make a list. On one side of a page, list what you like about your work and on the other side what you don't like. Analyze carefully what you feel. This may be hard to dig out or it may be quite obvious. Disregard any feelings that are negative only because the design did not measure up to your preconceived ideas of how it should look. This analysis should evaluate only what it is—on it's own merits.

## Design

If, in your evaluation of your picture, you end up with comments such as "I don't like the way it feels but I don't know why," you may need more information about design. Design is organization. To create a design you organize the components into an orderly composition. You take the parts or the building blocks and arrange them. These parts are color, line, form, area, and texture.

Color is a design component that holds much fascination and perhaps some confusion. We react to color according to our own personal life experiences, and there is no universal or right or wrong way to perceive color. I encourage freeing yourself from formula methods of viewing color and allowing your personal reactions to prevail. Most of us share some basic color perceptions that can be useful in color design. The sun and fire are usually seen as orange, yellow, and red, so we consider these to be "warm" colors. Atmospheric diffusion mutes and softens colors, so grayed colors appear farther away than bright, intense colors. For different seasons, nature provides a change of colors. These colors, however, can be very different for those who live in the Arctic as opposed to those who live in a tropical climate.

The study of color can be very exciting and can be directed in many specific areas. Whole university courses have been devoted to color as related to chemistry, physics, psychology, environment, light vision, and so forth. There are many scholarly studies, courses, and books that relate to color in art and design and even some specifically related to the textile arts. If, when you are viewing a fabric artwork, you have a strong reaction to the colors, analyze that reaction. Look closely and decide what it is about the colors you like or dislike. This will help you form your own personal guidelines when you are color designing.

Color is an important design tool. Approach it with a sense of adventure, freedom, and fun, and follow your heart for rewarding results.

Line is the design component that directs your eye. It delineates the edges of spaces and shapes, divides parts and forms, surrounds and defines the parts. It is the row of stitches formed by machine or by hand, or it may be a pencil or crayon mark that moves across a page. Line can also be created by a swath or band of color or texture that stands out against the background and directs the eye's movement through the composition.

Texture is an inherent component of fabric art. The word textile is intertwined with texture. The surface feel and appearance define the texture. Involved is not only feeling with the fingers or touch but also the visual feeling that prints and patterns present. The surface may feel or look bumpy, smooth, fuzzy, nubby, rough, prickly, harsh, soft, filmy, coarse, fluffy—an almost endless list of adjectives can be added. Both the touch and the visual texture are important in fabric designing.

Form and area are especially interesting terms. I like to visualize these two in this way. Form is an object or a positive shape, and area is the space around the form or the negative shape. To

create area, there must be a boundary. When you design a picture, the boundary is the outside edge or the frame. The size and shape of the picture defines the area. Being able to recognize the negative areas in a picture helps you control the design.

When you are arranging the building blocks or designing the picture, there also are several fundamentals that help you with organization. These are balance, rhythm, contrast, unity, proportion and scale.

Balance is an important fundamental to our well being both physically and visually. If you have the sensation that the composition leans to one side or is top heavy or affects your equilibrium (makes you nauseous), it probably needs balance adjustment. Check through the building block list. Is there a balance of color, line, form, area, and texture? Would it look better if there were more or less of any of these elements? For example, with a bright spot of red on one side, you may want one or two smaller red spots on the other side to balance the picture.

Rhythm is also referred to as repetition. Repeating a color, a line, or a shape develops rhythm in a design. Good design achieves a sensitive balance between enough variation to make the design interesting and enough repetition to set up a rhythm that carries the eye comfortably throughout the composition.

Contrast, or emphasis, creates a center of interest. Does your eye zap to one spot in the picture, or do you keep searching for something to focus on? Emphasis is achieved by working with tensions such as light against dark, large against small, wide against narrow, straight against curved or wiggly. If most of the picture has large, smooth, flat shapes and you throw in a small, jagged, highly textured spot, that spot immediately becomes the center of interest.

Unity or harmony means how well things go together. Using colors that are related on the color wheel creates unity. The background fabric on your picture is a unifying factor. When you use black thread for detailing the whole picture, that will unify the composition. Unity or harmony in design leaves the viewer with the feeling that nothing more needs to be added or taken away. Unity is a feeling of completeness.

Proportion and scale can be considered together. They involve the relationship of one part to another in amount or size. You may have heard reference to human scale, which is how people relate to objects in their environment. Have you ever felt overwhelmed by the towering mass of large skyscrapers in a city or by the sheer rock cliffs of a deep canyon? We become uncomfortable in a life space that is difficult to relate to because the proportion and scale are not quite right. A fine-textured, filmy, sheer, smooth fabric may not relate well to a coarse, rough burlap. Distance can be established by using scale. In a landscape the trees that are close appear larger than those farther away. We relate to our usual experiences in our visual world and become uncomfortable when things appear different.

No analysis would be complete without a discussion of mood. What feelings do the parts convey to you? First check the overall impact. Although this is largely dependent on your own personal past experiences, there are many universal feelings that the design components can convey. Bright, intense color is active; soft, diffused colors are quiet. Red, orange, and yellow are the colors of the sun and therefore are warm in feeling. A sharp, jagged line is active; a smooth, curving line is calming. If the composition lulls you to sleep or jangles your nerves and you wanted the opposite effect, try to decide what makes you feel that way. Sensitizing yourself to be aware of what you see and feel not only makes you a better designer, but also a better consumer and all around a more alive person.

Try the check list below to help you be a design sleuth. Ask yourself: Are the colors balanced? Do they create rhythm? Is there contrast? Are the colors

| | Balance | Rhythm | Contrast | Unity | Proportion and Scale | Mood |
|---|---|---|---|---|---|---|
| Color | | | | | | |
| Line | | | | | | |
| Form | | | | | | |
| Area | | | | | | |
| Texture | | | | | | |

unified, in proportion and scale? Do they create the mood you intended? Ask the same questions about line, form, area, and texture. You should not feel that you have to fill in all the blanks. Just one "Ah-hah" is a victory.

There is certainly a language of art and design. For some of us words and verbalization make the most sense; for others the feeling or a sense of right is more important. The ability to appreciate both viewpoints can be handy. Most of us have a bundle of preprogrammed attitudes and ideas that tend to limit our confidence and achievement. We were told at an early age what things should look like, and often we were ridiculed if they did not measure up. We locked in the images, and when we matured beyond them, the images were still there. Then we became our own worst critic, always striving towards someone else's visualization instead of our own.

When you are immersed in a new learning experience, as you are when learning how to make your sewing machine draw lines on cloth, you can more easily break free. The total concentration is a big help in getting rid of those self-imposed restrictions. Allow yourself to see with new clarity and to draw and reproduce images with confidence and pleasure. This will open the door to a whole new world of excitement. When you focus on the process you will more easily slip into the new viewpoint.

This is why I encourage you not to pencil a single line to follow on the fabric. Instead, place the pencil drawing idea beside you and follow the contours and lines with your eyes to draw with the sewing machine. When you do this, you will be concentrating on one section at a time. Instead of thinking this is what a cat looks like, you will look closely and see how the cat's ears meet the background. You will become aware of both positive and negative shapes. Making this visual and mental switch will help you create wonderful pictures, and you will be amazed at your new ability.

## Fabric—The Art "Material"

Just as important as the visualization and the sketch of your artwork is the choice of fabrics. The wonderful part of creating with fabric is the fabulous array of colors, textures, patterns, and weights available to us. Even if you were to limit your choices to only white fabrics, you would still have a large selection. You could find sheer, satin, muslin, corduroy, velvet, suede, fur fabric, linen, silk, white-on-white prints and many more. With only white to work with, all that variation would give you the opportunity to create a beautiful composition. Add color, and the choices multiply immeasurably.

Some fabrics can be manipulated to give a whole new effect. If you consider both the front and back of printed fabrics, you will discover subtle shade differences or even whole new color effects. Corduroys and velvets are a joy to work with. When you change the direction of the pile or nap, light reflection creates exciting color changes. I made a soft picture of corduroys and velvets depicting Idaho's Palouse in the winter (see photo of Jane's Winter View on page 37). The light reflection produces an ever-changing scene. As you walk past the picture, the changing angle of light reflection produces an effect of sunlight moving across the landscape. The whole picture changes color and mood from sunny days to cloudy, from morning to night and even from season to season.

Be brave in your fabric search and venture out of your usual section in the fabric shops. Examine all types of fabric for color, texture, and design. Be aware that texture is not only something you feel with your fingers but also something you feel with your eyes.

There are many times when creating fabric art that a fabric will provide the inspiration for the whole picture. You may look at a particular fabric, and it will bring all sorts of wonderful images to mind. When I saw a fabric that looked like rain or snow streaking across a gray sky, I was reminded of a favorite window seat in my childhood home. This was a place I spent many happy hours reading and sharing time with my dolls and teddy bear. I still have that wonderful old bear in his Oshkosh overalls and my baby doll in her lace dress and bonnet. So using these two as models, and adding others from memory, I created my soft picture "Storytime" (see photo on page 33).

CHAPTER 7

# All That Fabric

## The Fabric Stash

I hope you are now beginning to look at fabrics in a whole new light. There are so many exciting fabrics, and they can be used many ways. You can find great clouds and skies in any color combination imaginable; water, sandy beaches, forests, mountains, foggy vistas, pebbles, rocky crags, weathered boards, brick siding—anything you want. The key is to open your mind and look creatively. Train your eye to see beyond the printed design to what it can become. It is such fun to do. I often get some very strange looks in the fabric shops when I exclaim with glee "there—that is a

perfect jar of cherries!" and I am holding a dark red polka dot (see Harvest Jewels photo here and on page 38). I constantly search for unusual looks and textures that I have to have because I know I will use them sometime—somewhere! Doesn't that sound like a consummate fabriholic? Now I have given you a brand new approach and excuse for haunting the fabric shops!

## Fabric Storage

By now you have discovered lots of great excuses to bring those fabrics home with you. All of these exciting finds have been unloaded in the sewing space so you can dash off to find some more. Soon they begin to pile up and take over the house. When you decide to use that one "just right" piece that you bought last year in Port Orchard, Washington, you spend hours searching through the piles, and it is nowhere to be found! This is a familiar scenario, believe me, and because I feel just a tad guilty for having encouraged you to go on this fabric acquisition binge, I will share with you my solution. What is needed is a fabric filing and retrieval system. I will tell you about mine so you can, if you wish, adapt it to suit your needs.

## The Movable Studio

During the last several years my family has moved a lot—in fact eight times in five years. All during these moves I have had magazine deadlines to meet that required I send, for each issue, a soft picture and the instructions for making it. Knowing where to find everything that I needed to continue production became critical. With each move I was faced with creating a brand new work space. Creatively planning ahead and "making do" made survival possible. I am proud to say I have not missed a single

Polka Dot Fabric Used in Harvest Jewels Quilts

deadline, although some pretty creative mailing and delivery systems have come into play over the years.

Because I use both small and large fabric pieces in a variety of fabric types, I needed to create a fabric storage system that was well organized and eliminated time spent going through stacks of fabric. I also needed a system to work independently and on its own instead of being part of the room or sewing space. The space changed much too often, and I needed to find things fast. What I discovered that works well for me is a bazzillion boxes. Actually the last count by a disgruntled box-moving husband was 65. The boxes I use are about 12" x 15" x 10", and each has a separate cover. I managed to beg for and collect them from print shops and offices that use copy paper in large quantities.

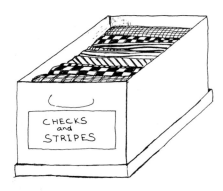

A box of this type is also available in knock-down form, sold for file or document storage. I label these boxes on both ends with large letters that list the contents. Think of it as a fabric filing system, with each box holding one group of fabrics in your fabric stash. I fold the fabrics to about 10" x 10" and place them in boxes on end with folded edge up. This allows you to run your hand down the on-edge stack of fabric and readily see what is there. To make selection even easier, I try to arrange the fabrics in a rainbow array of color families. For example, my box of sheer fabrics is divided into two parts: One half is nets and the other half is everything else. Then these are arranged red, orange, yellow, green, blue, purple, white, and black. The box is labeled SHEERS in large letters on each end. All of these boxes sit on open shelves, and when I hunt for fabrics, I lift the boxes down and pull out the types and colors I need. When each project is completed, the leftover fabrics are filed back in the appropriate boxes.

I use a lot of small pieces of plain (not patterned) fabrics in all colors for my pictures. For these I need a way to stack little pieces in color families on open shelves to be easily visible. My solution is cardboard shelf trays—the kind you find in office supply stores. They lie flat, have an open end, and stack one on top of another. Usually they store papers, pamphlets, or magazines. I fold the small pieces of

fabric and stack the pieces, folded side out, in the boxes. I arrange the fabrics in color families, and the boxes are arranged on the shelf in rainbow order. Besides making it easy for me to select the "just right" color, this box system makes a decorative display on the open shelves. For moving, these smaller boxes of fabric are stacked into larger cartons, open ends visible, and labeled for content and color.

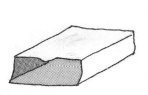

All of these boxes of fabric add up to a lot of weight—just ask my family during a move! I need a very sturdy shelf system to hold them. On every move, the room or space that I have available is very different. Sometimes I have a lovely big room with tall and long walls; other times only a closet or a hallway or an end of some other room. Once I even had to work from a mini-storage unit while we were between houses! The well-labeled box system is wonderful, and sturdy shelves are a must.

Murphy's law states that whenever you have a stack of boxes to the ceiling, the one you need is always on the bottom. I have devised a shelf system that works for me. I use decorative cinder blocks about 12" square and 4" deep for supports, and 2 x12's either four or eight feet long for shelves. The 2" thickness insures there will be no sag or collapse from the

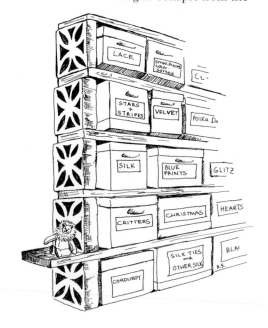

weight. I can usually find some wall that I can build the shelves against, or even use several half-walls. Floor to ceiling walls are my favorite—it is all there to scan at once—and feel smug about. This fabric storage system did take a while to organize and set up, but now that it is operational, I save hours of searching.

To round out this portable sewing capsule, all of my equipment and gear have their own packing containers, which also act as room furniture where possible. Tools and notions reside in a set of "boxes" that have their own knock-down metal shelves. Some of these have drawers, some drop fronts. They are labeled for content (pins, needles, buttons, etc.) and are easily accessible. When it's time to move, a piece of fiberfil goes in the top of each drawer and shelf, and an elastic band snaps over the whole box to hold it closed, and the boxes move as is. Each item has its own home, which is also the packing container. Although the actual placement in our new home may change, the constantly labeled container makes everything easily locatable. I have hooks screwed into wooden boards that I hang tools on. These fit into flat boxes with the tools still attached. Layers of fiberfil over the tools keep them from shifting. (Wonderful stuff, that stuffing!) The packing material is a reusable commodity. The success of the system is that the packing cartons are the furniture for the studio and lots of labeling makes it work. When everything has a place in the furnishings instead of the space, the trauma of forever searching is reduced a lot.

As with any filing system, this fabric storage system only works with careful use. Leftover pieces from each project should be returned to their place when each project is completed. New acquisitions need to find their home as soon as they arrive. Of course a "to be filed" box is a must, and occasionally new boxes need to be added or old ones rearranged. I always try to rearrange rather than add new so I can avoid that inevitable question "You have HOW many boxes of fabric to move?"

Another important part of the fabric creation operation for me is my worktable. In many new houses, I have had to be pretty creative to devise an

adequate work-surface solution. The challenge is to find a place that does not interfere with meal preparation and serving, and that does not block necessary passageways to the laundry or to the bathroom. Those wonderful tables that collapse into a tidy little capsule are great until you open one up to use it in that closet-sized "spare room" that is already furnished with a daybed and other necessities.

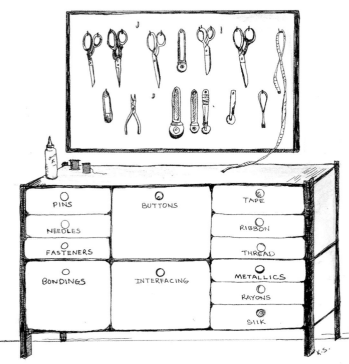

My solution was to use the space occupied by the guest bed. I had a piece of finished plywood cut to a size that will straddle the bed, and I purchased screw-in legs. Found in most hardware stores, these legs consist of a plate that is attached permanently to the underside of the table top at each corner plus the four legs. You can set your table up over the bed or daybed or even a sofa. When guests arrive, you unscrew the legs and store table top and legs under or behind the bed. This multiple use of occasionally used space has saved me from much family grumbling about fabric piled on chairs and sideboards, or threads in the soup.

I have talked about some of my strategies and methods to show you that for every situation there is a solution—one that is just right for you. A well-organized system and space can operate under adverse conditions and can, in the long run, save you a lot of time usually wasted by frantic searching. You can then direct your energies to being that creative person that is in each and every one of us.

# CHAPTER 8

# Making a Soft Picture

This book is dedicated to encouraging you to try stitching free. Now that you have found that free spirit within you, and are enjoying the free-motion straight-stitch drawing method, you are ready to make your first wonderful creation on your own. In this chapter I will walk you through the general steps that I usually follow when I make a soft picture. I will list tools and materials, discuss methods, and give hints, ideas and guidelines. You may wish to follow the whole process through as outlined, or follow just parts and pieces, or discard the whole thing and go your own way.

After this step-by-step process, you will find directions and patterns for three soft pictures in Chapter 9. These are included to illustrate different approaches to assembly and different materials and methods to use. I hope that these more specific instructions will help to clarify some of the procedures. This additional section is meant as an aid to your creative development. Remember that the fun and excitement of creating fabric art comes primarily from trying, experimenting, and discovering the methods, materials, and procedures that are right for you. Be sure, above all, to continue to nurture your new-found confidence, freedom, and adventurous spirit.

## The Process Step by Step

There are many ways to design with fabric and machine thread drawing. You can cut out precise pattern pieces and appliqué them to the background according to a planned design. You can cut the appliqué pieces free hand and apply them to the fabric, designing as you go. You can use free-motion straight stitches to attach the raw-edged pieces to the background and stop there. Or you might continue to detail and draw over the fabric. You can also use the free-motion straight stitches only (with no fabric appliqué) to machine draw your design. Whatever your favorite method of working with fabric, free-motion straight stitch can be incorporated in some way.

The steps that I follow when I make a soft picture are:

**Step 1**: Design

**Step 2**: Choose Fabric

**Step 3**: Cut Out Pieces

**Step 4**: Assemble

**Step 5**: Sew Down

**Step 6**: Detail

**Step 7**: Finish

**Step 8**: Enjoy!

You can jump in or back out at any point in the process, as you wish, but please always include Step 8—Enjoy!

## STEP 1: DESIGN

### Collect:
Sketch paper; pencils; eraser; ideas; dream time; idea clippings; tracing paper; optional—a light table.

### Procedure:
Rough sketch your ideas and develop a design. Simplicity of design and shape will make a first project more fun. Pencil draw your idea the size of your finished piece and draw in details. Color or write in color ideas. Pin up and admire; make changes if needed. Place tracing paper over your drawing and trace it again. You can eliminate detailing on this drawing but show the placement and the shapes of the appliqué pieces.

## Hint:
- A light table will make it easier to trace the shapes and lines and place the pieces, but tracing paper also works well.

## STEP 2: CHOOSE FABRIC

### Collect:
A base fabric; appliqué fabrics; scissors; optional—rotary cutter and mat.

### Procedure:
Choose a fabric for the base (the foundation you build the picture on). This will give you the body and the stability for stitching. It can become the background for your picture or you may use it for the sky and cover the rest with trees and hills, or you may cover the whole base piece with other fabrics. Cut the base fabric a minimum of 3" larger each direction than the finished picture will be (for an 18" x 20" picture, cut the fabric 24" x 26").

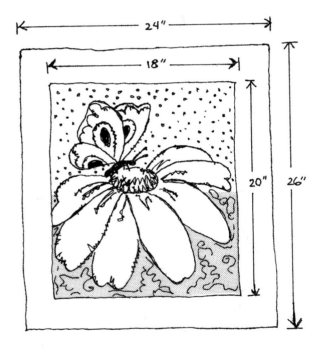

Place the base fabric on a table or on a wall with the drawing (detailed) beside it. This step can be called auditioning fabrics. Collect fabrics you may use and, folding them for approximate proportions, pin or place them on the base fabric. For very small spots of fabric, cut snippets to try out colors. Try different ones until you are satisfied with the combinations.

### Hint:
- As I choose my fabrics, I place them in a "working box" and put away the ones I have discarded. This helps eliminate confusion and clears the workspace.

## STEP 3: CUT OUT PIECES

### Collect:
Sharp scissors with long and short blades; glass-headed straight pins; a fabric glue stick; fusible bonding; fusible interfacing; dissolvable or tear-away stabilizers; optional—rotary cutter and mat.

### Procedure:
Place the base fabric on a work surface. Have the pencil drawing nearby. Place the tracing paper drawing over the base fabric. Cut out the appliqué pieces using any one or a combination of these methods.
1. Eyeball and cut free-hand (this works well for large pieces and amorphous shapes).
2. If the fabric is light-colored and thin, you can lay the fabric over the tracing paper drawing and trace off the outline directly onto the fabric, then cut out.
3. Trace a pattern piece on a fresh piece of tracing paper, pin this pattern to the fabric and cut it out.
4. Reverse the tracing paper picture (turn it over). Place paper-backed fusible bonding over the outline you want and trace it off on the fuse-bond paper. Bond this to the back of your appliqué fabric and cut the piece out.

Add to background in numbered order:
1. flower
2. center
3. back wing
4. front wings

### Hints:
- It is wise to stabilize small pieces and easily frayed fabrics. Fusible bonding will do this, or if you don't want a full bond, use fusible interfacing on the back of the appliqué piece.
- Pre-plan your cut pieces for overlaps. Nature is a good guide—the closest objects rest on top of those farther away. Trying to fit pieces of fabric by butting them together is a real pain. Overlap whenever possible. Also, layer smaller pieces on top of larger ones rather than cutting away underneath. For example, with flower centers, cut the whole flower and layer the fabric for the center on top. When cutting landscape-like pieces, cut them with

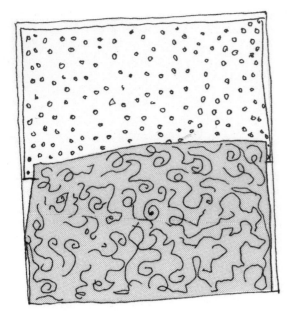

- If there is a definite layering to the picture, as in a scene with a window and foreground objects, I find it easier to do the stitching down for each layer, then add the next.
- When light-colored fabrics overlap bright or dark-colored fabrics, the color underneath will show through as a shadow. If this is not desirable, trim away the underlap to ⅛" or less when placement is certain.

generous underlaps. You can trim away excess after you have assembled them.

- When you cut out pieces that go to the edge of your picture (for example a sky piece), cut them long enough to fit right out to the edge of your base fabric (all three extra inches). This will save you grief with fabric gaps later.
- Do not cut up your pencil drawing or the tracing paper drawing to use as pattern pieces. You will need both of these for assembly and finishing.

## STEP 4: ASSEMBLE

### Collect:

Glass-headed straight pins; your choice of fabric glue stick or fusible bonding materials.

### Procedure:

Place base fabric on a work surface and pin the traced drawing to the top edge of the base fabric so it can be lifted up. Lift up the tracing paper, place the cut fabric piece on the backing, lower the tissue and adjust the placement to match the drawing. Pin in place. If there is a background (such as sky and hills) behind foreground objects, arrange all the background pieces first, then arrange the foreground pieces. The background pieces should go completely behind the foreground pieces instead of cutting away. It may be easier to assemble small pieces by tucking them under larger pieces after the larger one is in position. For example, place a flower, then tuck leaf ends and stem ends under the flower. When all pieces are pinned in place, remove the tissue drawing and stand back and admire. Readjust placement where needed. Trim off extra underlap when you are certain of the placement. Pin, glue, or fuse in place to prepare for sewing down.

## STEP 5: SEW DOWN

### Collect:

Sewing machine in free-motion straight-stitch mode; thread nippers or scissors; sewing thread that matches or blends with the appliqué pieces; needles that go with the threads; a chalk marking tool or disappearing marker; ruler and square.

### Procedure:

Sew each piece of appliqué fabric to the base fabric using a matching or blending thread color. How securely you sew it down depends on the use it will receive and also how much detail stitching you have planned. This step is to hold the patches in position so you will have much more freedom of motion when you detail the picture. Once around will secure the patches in place; two or three times will ensure that you catch all the edges and that you will smooth and blend the edge line. These stitches should follow the edge of each shape. When everything is tacked down, pin your creation up on the wall, stand back and admire. At this time you can add or subtract patches where needed. Using your paper drawing as a guide, draw a chalk line on your fabric picture indicating the outside finished edge of your picture. This line will help you visualize the edge of your work while you are detailing. I suggest a non-permanent chalkline because these edges may change position as the picture progresses.

## Hints:

- If the appliqué pieces are large and have smooth edges that do not require frequent direction changes, you may want to sew the patches down using regular feed-through stitching. For small patches with ziggy edges, free stitch is much easier.
- You can use a transparent or see-through thread for this step. It will avoid having to change the thread color for each fabric color (this is your choice, of course).
- An advantage of picture making by collage-type assembly is that if you do not like the way a sewn-down piece of fabric looks, you can cover it with something else. Just position the new patch over the old one and stitch it in place.

## STEP 6: DETAIL

### Collect:

Sewing machine in free-motion, straight-stitch mode; special threads and matching needles; black or other contrasting colored thread; paper drawing of the picture showing details; and clippings for detail scrutiny.

### Procedure:

This is the fun, free-wheeling, creative stage of the picture-making process. This is where your new machine-drawing skills come into play. With everything secured in position you have in front of you a playground for free stitching. Prop up the paper drawing of your picture and any clippings and photos so they are handy to look at while you sew.

The first step is to decide where you might want to use different colored threads for details and what colors you will use. You may decide to use white or light-colored thread to create highlights, or dark colors for shadows. You can create details such as thistle flowers ("Blue Gossamer Wings," see photo on page 40), flower centers ("Flite of Flowers," see photo on the back cover), eyes, leaf veins, fur or fuzz, or small spots of color ("March Winds, April Showers," see photo on page 40) with thread. This is a good time to add special thread touches by using metallics, rayons, silks, or heavier threads. On areas of black or dark-colored fabric, use light colors or white for details. With your decision made, thread the machine and start to play. I love this part! Think good thoughts,

play and doodle, relax and enjoy. Every once in a while, stop, stand back, and admire your progress.

When you have completed the color thread additions, it is time for the final detailing. I like to use black thread for this but you might choose another color. This step gives the finishing touch to your art work. The black thread is a cohesive force, the visual glue that binds it all together and brings it into focus. When you want something to stand out, a fine line of contrasting color will give it an edge and define it. Take a deep breath, relax, dive in, and play. Draw over, define, and create new shapes with this wonderful drawing tool, your sewing machine. Keep the motion smooth and the action free. Usually you will enjoy the line more if you forget the exact edge of the fabric pieces and draw outside and inside the shapes. A free, fluid line that redefines the shape is more interesting. If you do not like the first line, go around again, and a third time; this will average out the line direction. Every now and then, stop and admire from a distance. Each time decide, "Should I stop or do more?" If you let your eyes "listen," they will tell you when the picture is finished. When it is complete, hang it where you can look at and admire it as you pass by several times a day. Isn't it wonderful? You should be proud!

There is one more free-motion sewing task before your artwork is completed. That is to sign your name. Be sure to choose a place that will not be trimmed off or hidden by framing, and give your creation that final touch.

## Hints:

- If you try to make a perfectly straight line when sewing in the free-motion straight-stitch mode, you will be disappointed. Go for the creative line; you will be amazed how much better it will look.
- Remember to put the presser foot down when stitching. It is easy to forget and causes all sorts of looping, knotting, and snarling (both the thread and you).
- Keep your fingers out from under the needle—no bleeding on masterpieces allowed!

## STEP 7: FINISH

### Collect:

T-square; ruler; triangle; chalk marker; scissors and/or rotary cutter and mat; backing fabric; filler; optional— half picture mats (two L-shaped mat pieces); reducing glass or camera viewfinder.

### Procedure:

Your wonderful picture is completed—but not quite. You owe it to your creation and yourself to get it into presentable form—to finish it. You may decide to

frame it with a rigid frame, or sew on a border for a soft finish.

I like to finish my pictures with a soft frame as I prefer the textile quality this accentuates. Many people that have my soft pictures have had them rigid-framed for visual impact and to protect them; and I am usually pleased with the way they look. Whatever you decide, you will need to square the picture off again to prepare it for finishing. If you have used extra fabric for your base piece and have carried the appliqué pieces to the outside edges as suggested, you now have extra fabric to work with. The machine drawing has probably caused some distortion and you will need to realign the edges. You can choose to make your picture larger or smaller than originally planned or move it to the right, left, up, or down.

To make a decision on the new edges, I find it helpful to use cardboard (mat board) strips or right-angle L-shaped pieces. Lay these over the picture edges and move them around until you like the picture you see. Other tools I have used to help make this decision are a reducing glass and the viewfinder on a camera. A reducing glass is the opposite of a magnifying glass, making everything you see through it look smaller. If you look at your picture through the viewfinder on your camera, you will see it smaller and also "framed." When you have decided where the edges will be, mark one side. Next, check right angles and mark the other three sides, making sure the opposite ones are parallel. Mark the edges $1/4$" out from where you want the finished edge. This way you will be sure the mark won't show when the mat or fabric frame is added.

If you plan to rigid-frame the piece, decide the method and leave enough fabric for any wrap-around or matting. Trim away the excess. When making a border and soft finishing, I like to allow $1/2$" or more for the seam, so I will trim $1/4$" outside of the markings.

Choose compatible border fabric(s) and sew on, mitering or butting the corners as desired. I have found that a soft picture hangs better and lies flatter if it has some body or filler. For this I have used several different types of materials. For a slim look, a single layer of a thin fleece-type filler works well. Sometimes I will use two or even three layers, or a thin quilt batting. The thin materials give a flatter effect; the thicker layers create a more pouffy, padded look. The picture sandwich, just like a quilt, consists of three layers. Your picture with the border is the top layer; the filler is the middle layer; and you will need a backing fabric for the bottom layer.

Cut the backing fabric and the filler larger than the top by a minimum of $1/2$" on each side. This allows for quilting distortion. Place the backing on a flat surface, wrong side up. Layer the filler on the backing, then the top, smoothing each layer. Pin or baste these layers together and you are ready to quilt by hand or machine. Quilting secures the layers and reduces sagging. The quilting stitches will also add texture and design and can counteract distortion. I usually follow the outlines of the major appliqué pieces in the picture for the quilting, and the seams in the border.

Resquare the corners and straighten the edges when quilting is completed. Sew on a binding if desired, or fold the border fabric over the edge to the back and hand sew in place.

## Hints:

- If you are having your fabric picture framed, be sure your framer is aware of care precautions when framing textiles. Acid-free materials should be used to prevent deterioration. If glass is used, the fabric should not touch the glass, both for appearance and for care of the fabric. Fabric pieces need to breathe when in a frame so that harmful chemicals do not build up.

- A thick quilt batting used as a filler for a small picture generally will distort the fabric. Your soft picture may end up looking like a soft sculpture. If you planned it, this may actually be fun, although hard to control.

- Sometimes I plan ahead for areas where I want texture and dimension to be developed by the quilting stitches. Stipple quilting and other all-over textures can be interesting additions to machine-drawn art. Quilted clouds ("March Winds, April Showers," see photo on page 40) or furrow lines in fields ("Palouse Hills Quilt," see photo on page 36) can add a whole new look to the design.

## STEP 8: ENJOY!

### Collect:

Collect a happy heart, a sense of humor, and a few good friends.

### Procedure:

Hang your picture in a prominent place to admire and enjoy. With such a wonderful sense of accomplishment, you should feel very proud.

### *Hint*:

- Believe in yourself, follow your heart, create with enthusiasm and a sense of humor. Everyone will enjoy your creation—especially you!

You have now discovered the thrill and excitement of creating fabric images. No matter how you adapt the information and pursue the method, your results will be rewarding. Remember that success is in every step achieved. Enjoy the doing and always be proud of your accomplishments.

# CHAPTER 9

# Three Patterns To Try

The three patterns in this chapter include full-size pattern pieces and instructions so that you can try some of the skills and techniques you have learned for free-motion straight-stitch pictures before you set out on your own. Each picture pattern gives you a chance to practice different new skills. Unless directed to do otherwise, you will not need to add seam allowances to any of the appliqué pieces.

It is important to notice the difference between the words "sew" and "detail" when you are doing free-motion straight-stitch pictures. In most cases you will first "sew" a shape in place by using a neutral or matching-colored thread to sew along the edges of the shape. This can be the on/off line technique where you don't always follow the exact edge of the shape or it may follow the edge line exactly. Detailing is usually done after a shape has been sewn in place, and a contrasting or brighter or darker thread is used to define the edges of the shape as well as sections or parts inside or outside of the shape. You may want to use some of the shapes and fill-in lines that you learned on the Doodle Page (page 14) or create other styles of your own. But do notice the difference between sewing and detailing as you follow the directions for the three picture patterns.

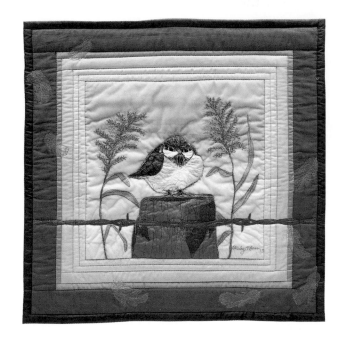

## Pattern No. 1: Our Feathered Friend

*Finished Size: 25″ x 25″. Inspiration for this soft picture came from a pen-and-ink drawing made by my daughter-in-law, graphic artist Jackie Nilsson. This quilt is shown in color on page 47.*

### This pattern illustrates:

- Overlapping sheer fabrics for a "watercolor" look.
- Using sheers for shadows (on the post).
- Pre-detailing a "patch" (the bird) and then adding it to the picture.
- "Framing" with multi-colored strips color-keyed to the background colors.
- Spilling the picture into the frame (wire and feathers).

## Collect Materials:

- Base Fabric: A bright-white 18" square
- Background and Border Feathers: A collection of sheer fabrics (fine net, organdy, organza, chiffon, etc.), 18" long by 2" to 10" wide in light blue, pink, violet, white, peach, purple; ¾ yard of peach illusion (fine-net) veiling.
- Bird: An 8" square of white-on-white print cotton; small scraps of peach-colored chiffon, gray-brown organdy, black fine-mesh net.
- Grasses and Post: ¼ yard brown cotton (for post and wire); ¼ yard gray/brown organdy (for grasses and shadow); scrap of white fine-mesh net (for highlights on post).
- Borders: Approximately ¼ yard each of six cotton fabrics that echo the colors in the sheer background colors—light peach, medium peach, light blue-purple, light red-purple, medium-dark purple, dark red-purple.
- Filler and Backing: 30" square of thin quilt batting; 30" square of backing fabric of your choice.
- Threads: Cotton and/or rayon thread in brown, light beige, dark brown, white, peach, yellow, and gray.

## Procedure:

### Background Grasses and Sheers (First Layer):

1. On the white 18" square base fabric, mark the picture's final size (15" x 15") in the center.
2. Pattern pieces are found on the pullout at the back of this book. For the background layer, trace and cut the grass heads and leaf shapes from gray/brown organdy. Free-form cut two stems approximately 10" x ¼" from the same organdy. Position these "cut" grass and leaf shapes plus the stems on the base fabric and sew down with matching thread.
3. Cut pieces of sheer fabrics 18" long in varying free-flowing shapes from 2" to 10" wide. Starting at the top of the picture with purple sheers, layer and overlap the pieces. Tone from purples through blues to peach at the bottom of the picture. Cover the entire base fabric, including the grasses, too. When satisfied with the color blend, sew the sheers down with a neutral-colored thread in horizontal lines across the picture, following the color edges.

### Post and Stitched Grasses (Second Layer):

1. Pattern pieces are found on the pullout at the back of this book. Cut post out of brown cotton. Cut shadow shapes from gray/brown organdy and highlight shapes from white net. Position and pin all patches in place. Sew all patches down with brown thread.
2. Cut an 18" x 18" piece of peach-colored illusion veiling and cover the whole picture with it, pinning in place here and there.

Grass and Sheers (First Layer)

Post and Stitched Grasses (Second Layer)

65

3. With light beige thread, detail the grass heads, the stems and leaves, and the post. Use ziggy lines for the grass heads. With dark-brown thread, complete the detailing of the grasses and the post.

Bird and Border Placement

### The Bird:

1. In the center of the 8" square of white-on-white fabric, trace the bird outline (pattern pieces are found on the pullout at the back of this book). From peach-colored sheer fabric, cut four pieces for breast, one smaller and one larger piece for each side. From gray/brown organdy, cut the wing, head cap, and feet. From black fine-mesh net, cut eyes and neck patch. Position all patches on the bird outlined on the white-on-white fabric and pin in place.

2. Sew down pieces and detail in one step. Starting with white thread, surround the eyes and "feather" the neck patch and breast with ziggies. Use peach-colored thread to blend the breast pieces to each

other and to the white. With yellow thread, "color in" the beak with close-together ziggies. With brown thread, make the eye pupils, define the beak and feet, and shape the cheeks.

3. When the bird is complete, cut away the white-on-white fabric around the bird. Position the bird on the post. Sew down and then detail the edges with white and gray threads.

### Borders and Frame:

1. Cut the following strips from pastel cotton fabrics: From light peach cut two strips 1" x 15$\frac{1}{2}$" and cut two strips 1" x 16$\frac{1}{2}$". From medium peach, cut two strips 1" x 16$\frac{1}{2}$" and two strips 1" x 17$\frac{1}{2}$". From light blue-purple, cut two strips 1$\frac{1}{2}$" x 17$\frac{1}{2}$" and two strips 1$\frac{1}{2}$" x 19$\frac{1}{2}$". From light red-purple, cut two strips 1" x 19$\frac{1}{2}$" and two strips 1" x 20$\frac{1}{2}$". From medium-dark purple, cut two strips 2$\frac{1}{2}$" x 20$\frac{1}{2}$" and two strips 2$\frac{1}{2}$" x 24$\frac{1}{2}$". From dark red-purple cut two strips 1$\frac{1}{2}$" x 24$\frac{1}{2}$" and two strips 1$\frac{1}{2}$" x 26$\frac{1}{2}$".

2. Straighten the picture edges and trim to measure 15$\frac{1}{2}$" square. In the same color sequence as you cut fabric strips in Step 1 above (starting with the light peach), sew shorter strips of each color to the upper and lower edges of the picture; then sew longer strips to side edges (except for final dark red-purple ones).

3. Before attaching the final side strips, add the barbed-wire fence: From brown cotton, cut out the

barbed wire (pattern pieces are found on the pullout at the back of this book). Position and sew it in place with matching thread. Detail with a light gray thread to highlight the twists and coiled barbs.

4. Sew on the last two side border pieces. From peach-colored fine-mesh netting, cut out eight feathers and pin in place. With beige thread, sew down and detail the feathers in one step. Use circular squiggles to form the fuzzy parts of the feathers.

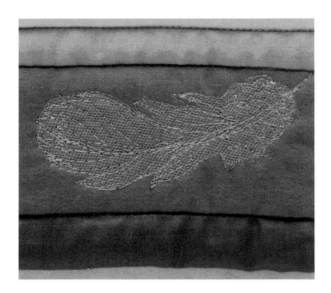

### Finishing:

1. Layer the backing fabric (face down), batting, and the finished picture (facing up). Pin or baste. Quilt around the bird, the post, the wire, and in-the-ditch along border seams. Do not quilt through the floating feathers. Trim backing and batting to $1/4$" smaller than the picture top on all sides. Fold front raw edge twice toward the back to form a folded edge on the back. Slipstitch in place.

## Pattern No. 2: Flite of the Flowers

*Finished Size: 22" x 27." This quilt is shown in color on the back cover.*

### This pattern illustrates:

- Building a picture in three stages: 1) the background, 2) blue flowers and leaves, and 3) daisies and butterflies.
- Using sheers and multi-colored threads (for the blue flowers).
- Free-hand cutting for background pieces.
- Spilling the picture onto the frame.

### Collect Materials:

- Base Fabric: $3/4$ yard of mottled blue-and-white fabric that looks like clouds; add iron-on interfacing (or lightly starch) if needed.
- Cottons: $1/2$ yard white; $1/4$ yard yellow; $1/4$ yard medium green; $1/4$ yard dark green, scrap of red.
- Sheer Fabrics: From organdy or chiffon, $1/4$ yard each of light blue, yellow, white, bright pink, light green, beige. From wide-mesh net, $1/4$ yard bright pink. From fine-mesh net, $1/4$ yard purple.
- Frame and Backing: $1/2$ yard dark blue print for frame; $2 1/4$ yards navy blue piping; 1 yard print for backing fabric; 28" x 33" thin batting; 3 yards navy blue bias quilt binding.
- Threads: Cotton and/or rayon thread in black, white, navy, yellow, light blue, bright blue, green, and pink.

## Procedure:

### The Background (first layer):

1. Cut base/background cloud fabric to 21" x 26", which allows an extra 3+" on all sides of the 15" x 20" picture. Use iron-on interfacing or add starch to the back if needed.
2. Using the approximate sizes of the shapes shown in the figure below, cut background shapes free-hand from dark green cotton, sheer light green organdy, beige sheer organdy, and pink wide-mesh net. Keep in mind that these are background pieces, which do not require an exact outline—rather they are approximate shapes.
3. Layer these background pieces in the order listed. Sew them down with a matching or neutral thread.

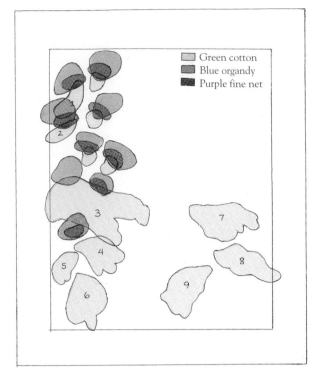

Blue Flowers and Leaves (Second Layer)

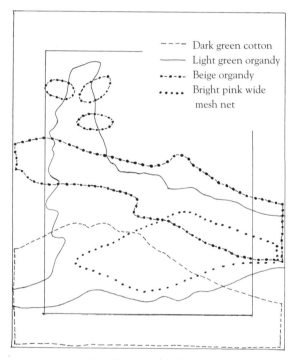

The Background (First Layer)

### Blue Flowers and Leaves (second layer):

1. Pattern pieces are found on the pullout at the back of this book. Cut flowers and leaves from medium green cotton (leaves and flower bases), light blue organdy (two flower shapes are provided—mix, match, and reverse as you please), and purple fine-mesh net (flower shading).
2. Position with leaves under and flower bases over sheer blue and purple. Purple is on top of blue. Sew down with matching thread. Use the free-motion straight stitch to create details and flower petals. Use pink, light blue, and bright-blue threads in long zigs and bird-claw shapes over the net and sheer.

3. Detail the leaves and bases with green thread. Finish the detailing on these pieces with black thread. Add light detailing with green and tan thread to the background foliage shapes sewn down earlier for background pieces.

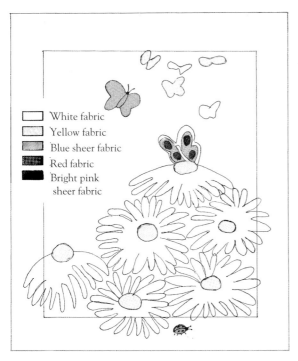

Legend:
- □ White fabric
- □ Yellow fabric
- ▨ Blue sheer fabric
- ▨ Red fabric
- ■ Bright pink sheer fabric

Daisies and Butterflies (Third Layer)

## Daisies and Butterflies (third layer):

1. Pattern pieces are found on the pullout at the back of this book. Stabilize the white and yellow cottons with light starch. From white cotton, cut five daisies and one 7" square for the sixth daisy. From yellow cotton, cut six daisy centers. From white sheer, cut one large butterfly and two small butterflies. From yellow sheer, cut three butterflies. From light-blue sheer, cut one butterfly and four butterfly wing spots. From pink sheer, cut four wing spots. From red cotton scrap, cut one ladybug.

2. Lightly trace the bottom center daisy on the 7" white square. Add the yellow center and sew down. Set aside the ladybug and the bottom center daisy on the 7" square, as these will go over the framing borders later.

3. Position the pieces (except for the bottom center daisy and ladybug). Place daisies and then yellow centers on top of them. Sew down with matching thread.

4. Layer the large butterfly with white on the bottom, then blue, then pink on top. Place smaller butterflies as pattern shows or as you wish. Sew down with matching thread.

5. With pink thread detail the daisy centers (including the one sewn onto the 7" white square) and large butterfly wings. With yellow thread, fill in yellow daisy centers with squiggles. With white thread, detail blue, yellow, and white small butterflies. Afterward, with black thread, detail the yellow butterflies, the petals on the five attached daisies, and large butterfly.

## Borders and Finishing:

1. From blue print, cut two strips 4" x 22$\frac{1}{2}$" and two strips 4" x 27$\frac{1}{2}$". From piping cut two pieces 15$\frac{1}{2}$" and two pieces 20$\frac{1}{2}$".

2. Realign and square edges of picture so that the finished picture line is 15" x 20"; mark that line; then mark and trim $\frac{1}{4}$" outside of finished picture line.

3. Place piping along finished picture line with raw edges away from picture, and sew down. Position print frame strips on all sides, and sew in place only to the seam lines. Miter corners.

4. Cut out, position, and sew lower daisy in place, detailing with black as you did for other daisies. Sew ladybug in place on lower framing strip and detail with black.

5. Layer backing (right side down), batting, and picture top (right side up). Baste or pin. Quilt layers (using thread color of your choice) together across from left to right in bands for the sky, around the outside edges of butterflies, all flower shapes, and leaves, flower bases, and daisy centers. Quilt in-the-ditch along piping seam and $\frac{1}{4}$" outside of piping around frame.

6. Trim backing and batting to match edges of picture top. Sew binding onto front of picture, roll it over to the back, and hand sew to finish.

69

## Pattern No. 3: Catch A Falling Star

*Finished Size: 45" x 45". My inspiration for this picture was the childhood song, "Catch a Falling Star and Put It in Your Pocket...Save It for a Rainy Day." This quilt is shown in color on page 41.*

### This pattern illustrates:

- Creating a background by sewing bands of cottons onto the base fabric to cover the entire surface.
- Using two colors of ribbon to make an overlying trellis.
- Making roses from print fabrics.
- Reshaping stars to fit skewed quilt squares.
- Blending background colors with random quilting lines.

### Collect Materials:

- Base Fabric: Approximately 50" square. This will be completely covered, so any medium-weight fabric will work, and it can be seamed if necessary.
- Background Fabrics: Twenty different cotton fabrics in strips of varying widths that are at least 52" long. The colors blend from deep navy at the top through rose, purple, mauve, pink, peach, and medium blues at the bottom. Use a variety of fabric types including pindots and polished cottons.
- Trellis: $7^1/2$ yards of $^5/8$"-wide white bias binding, 10 yards of $^3/8$"-wide white grosgrain ribbon, and 10 yards of $^3/8$"-wide gray satin ribbon; 6" square of white cotton for finial and shelves.
- Trellis Roses: $^1/4$ to $^1/2$ yard of cotton fabric printed with large roses (you'll need approximately 18 roses and buds altogether); 2 yards of $^1/4$"-wide gray-green fabric strips cut on the bias for vines; green scraps for approximately 25 leaves.
- Figures: Small scraps of prints and solid colors for hair, dresses, faces and hands, cats, basket, chair,

and stars. Use the color photograph on page 41 as a guide. Small piece of netting and 6" of $^1/8$"-wide red grosgrain ribbon for handle on star catcher.

- "Star" Quilt: $^1/2$ yard of navy blue pindot; $^1/2$ yard white cotton.
- Borders, Backing, and Filler: $1^3/8$ yards medium blue for border; $1^1/2$ yards of backing fabric; 50" square of thin quilt batting; 6 yards of navy blue bias quilt binding.
- Threads: Cotton and/or rayon thread in gray, white, and colors that match all horizontal background pieces, figures, stars, and Star quilt fabrics.
- Optional: An iron-on bonding product that fuses two pieces of fabric together works well for assembling small pieces in this picture.

### Procedure:

#### Background:

1. Cover the 50" square base fabric completely with long angular and undulating strips of the 20 different fabrics. These strips might have raw edges stitched down or they may be sewn together into one large piece with seams pressed, and then turned over to the right side. My method is to lay out these strips horizontally, turn under edges, and topstitch in place (see Step 2).

2. Starting at the top edge, place a navy pindot on the backing, covering the top and side edges of the base fabric. Lay the next strip overlapping the navy pindot a little higher than where the seam line will be. Mark an angular cutting line and trim both pieces. Turn the second (lower) piece under $^1/4$" on the top edge and move it up to overlap the first fabric by about $^1/4$". Pin securely over the first fabric and through the base fabric.

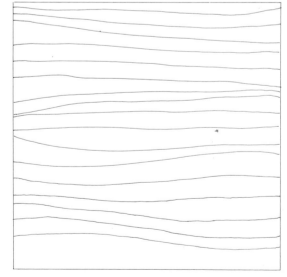

Background Layer

3. Continue in this manner for all 20 fabrics. When the last fabric is in place at bottom of picture, trim

away any excess level with the bottom of the base fabric. Also trim top and sides so edges are even with base fabric.

4. Topstitch all 20 fabrics in place using matching-colored thread and a regular sewing (feed-through) setting.

Trellis Overlay

**Trellis With Roses:**

1. On the background, mark a centered 45" square (Line A). With removable marker, mark Line B 2½" inside the 45" square along each side, top, and bottom. (The 45" line will be the outside edge of the border and binding; the inner line will be the outside edge of the trellis.)

2. Mark the inside trellis line (Line C) 4¼" inside at the side bases and curving up to 1" at the top center. Mark diagonal lines 1" apart between the two trellis lines in both directions.

3. Center the gray satin ribbon along the marked lines in one direction only (toward top center) and sew down on both long edges, trimming excess ribbon. Repeat with the white grosgrain ribbon in the other diagonal direction (away from top center).

4. Cut out finial (pattern pieces are found on the pullout at the back of this book) and sew in place at inside arch center. Cut out white trellis shelves and sew at two different levels, one along each inner side of trellis. Center white bias tape along the inside line of trellis (Line C), having the edge of the tape cover the ends of all ribbons, finial, and shelves. Sew in place on both edges of tape.

5. Trim background ¼" outside of Line B. From medium blue, cut four strips 2½" x 46". Sew a strip to the top and the two sides of quilt picture, stopping seam ¼" from each end of seam. Miter two top corners of this medium blue border.

6. Place white tape along inside border seams (Line B) at top and two sides, covering ribbon ends. Fold a miter at each upper corner. Sew in place on both edges of tape.

7. No seam allowances are required when you cut roses out of print fabric, leaves from green fabric, and vine from gray-green fabric cut on the bias. Arrange the vines on each side of the trellis and free-straight stitch them in place using matching thread. Add leaves and roses and sew in place. Detail the vines, leaves and roses with black thread.

8. Sew fourth medium-blue border to bottom edge, stopping seam ¼" from each end of seam and catching trellis and vine ends in the seam. Miter two bottom corners of border.

9. Detail finial and two white trellis shelves with gray thread.

71

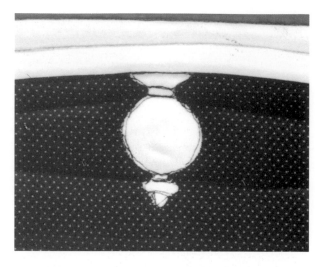

## Figures:

1. *Note:* All of these small pieces are more manageable if an iron-on bonding is used. Pattern pieces are found on the pullout at the back of this book. Trace and cut out all pieces without seam allowances. Assemble the figures before adding to the background picture. Tuck necks and wrists under dresses and place hair on top. To hold in place, touch tip of iron to pieces just enough to bond lightly.

2. For the Star Quilt, cut an 18" piece of white fabric. Cut the quilt shape from navy pindot and center on the 18" white square. Sew down with matching thread. With white thread, "draw" the lines forming the quilt block squares. To determine the skewed shapes of the stars for each block, lay a piece of tracing paper over the little quilt and trace off the squares. Draw stars in appropriate squares so that they follow the contours of these squares. Cut stars from a variety of colors and sew down, then detail with white thread.

3. Cut a thin strip of blue bias and sew on for a quilting frame hoop. Cut out the Star quilt shape along the blue pindot edge at the top but leaving a narrow white border edge at lower right side and bottom edges.

4. Assemble the three figures around the quilt. Place the chair seat under the dress and the chair back over the dress. On the background, position the three figures and the quilt. Tuck figures under and arms and hands over the quilt. Lightly press to bond in place.

5. Referring to the placement drawing on page 74, arrange all of the finished figures and stars on the background before sewing down to allow for shifts

**Finishing**

1. Layer the backing fabric (face down), the batting, and the finished picture top (face up). Baste or pin layers. Quilt randomly placed horizontal lines across the background sky. Do not quilt through the figures or the stars. Quilt in-the-ditch around all figures. Quilt in-the-ditch along each white ribbon trellis edge and along the white bias tape trellis edges. Trim and square the outside edges of the medium-blue border. Sew on navy quilt binding to finish.

and changes. Place the stars last. Lightly press to bond in place.

6. When upper right figure is positioned, cut net for the star catcher and a star. Place star under the net. Use a narrow red grosgrain ribbon for the handle.

7. Cut out stars in various colors and position in the basket (cut a curved slit and tuck stars inside), with the cats, and scattered through the sky. Sew figures and stars in place; then detail with contrasting thread.

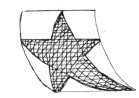

Shapes of Stars

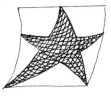

Placement of Figures and Stars

74

# CHAPTER 10

# A Method for Hanging Soft Pictures

Over the years, especially since I have had magazine deadlines, I have made a lot of soft pictures. I have finally devised a method for hanging them that is unobtrusive, easy to use, and it keeps the picture from drooping or curling. Because I am quite pleased with it, I thought I would share the idea with you. The method consists of a fabric sleeve, a flat wooden bar, and a screw-in picture ring.

## Collect:

1. Wooden piece, rectangular in cross-section, with all edges squared, measuring $1^1/2$" x $1/4$" x the length of the top of your picture. (I use wooden doorstop molding from a builders' supply house.)

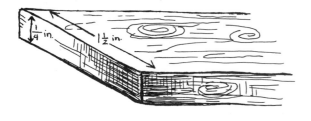

2. Screw-in decorative picture ring, medium size. These rings are used to hang lightweight wood-framed pictures and consist of a metal loop attached to a screw. Choose one that has a screw, which will turn into $1/4$"-thick wood without splitting the wood. These rings come in various sizes.

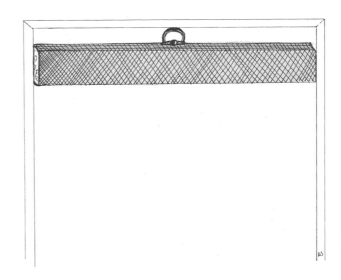

3. A piece of backing fabric that will cover the board.
4. An awl or drill to make a hole in the $1/4$" board for the screw to go into.

## Procedure:

1. Measure the top edge of the picture. Subtract $1/2$" from this measurement and cut the wooden piece that length. Sand the rough edges. Measure around the wooden piece ($1/4$" + $1^1/2$" + $1/4$" + $1^1/2$" = $3^1/2$"). To this measurement add the seam allowances plus $1/8$" slack ($3^1/2$" + $1/2$" + $1/8$" = $4^1/8$"). To the board length measurement add $1/4$" for a hem on each end ($1/2$" altogether). Cut a piece of backing the length of the board length measurement + hem x the width measurement around the wooden piece ($4^1_8$").

2. With wrong sides together, seam the fabric strip down the length to form a tube with the seam on the outside. Press the seam open and the tube flat with the seam in the center of the strip.

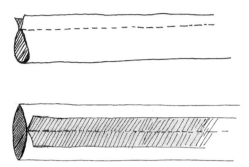

3. Place the wood strip centered over the seam and mark the fabric with a pencil line on both sides of the wood. Press the fabric tube again to remove the original press lines and make new creases on the pencil-marked lines.

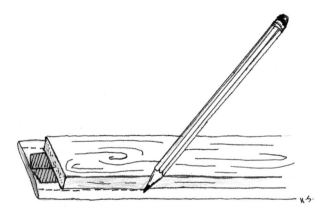

4. On the back of the picture, measure down from the top of the picture, the size of the hanging loop plus $1/8$" (so hanging loop doesn't show above picture). Mark a line all the way across the back of the picture at this level.

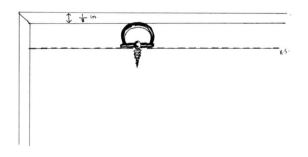

5. Pin the fabric sleeve (tube) to the back of the picture with the seam against the backing and matching the line on the backing with one crease line on the sleeve. Sew the two together by hand along this line, being careful that the stitches do not show on the front of the picture. Hand sew the other creased edge of the sleeve to the backing so that the sleeve lies flat covering the sleeve seam.

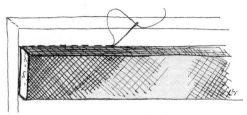

6. Slip the wooden piece into the sleeve. Find the center of the sleeve-covered wooden piece and mark. With the awl or a drill, make a hole through the sleeve fabric into the wood on the top $1/4$" side at the middle mark. Screw the hanging loop into this hole. Hang on the wall with a single hook or nail.

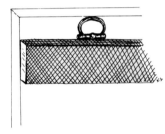

## Hints

- The flat, square-edged wooden piece attached this way allows the front of the picture to hang straight and flat. A round wooden piece or one where the sleeve does not allow slack for the thickness of the rod will cause a bulge on the front of the picture.

- When you wish to remove the wooden bar, unscrew the hanging loop and pull out the bar. To replace it, slide the bar back in, line up the fabric and wood holes, and screw the ring in.

# Glossary of Terms

**Background Fabric:**
The part of the picture that is behind the foreground parts. It is the fabric that remains visible in a picture upon which principal fabric shapes are placed. It can portray the sky or hills or grass or leaves or whatever items that form a setting for the foreground objects.

**Base Fabric:**
The piece of fabric that a soft picture is built upon. It may form the background or be completely covered by other fabric background pieces. It serves as a foundation to hold the fabric picture pieces.

**Bazzillion:**
A very large, indeterminate number.

**Bloop:**
A pouffed, puffed up, or raised portion on the fabric surface formed by stitching around and around a circular shape.

**Bonding:**
An iron-on product that is placed between two pieces of fabric and warmed by the iron. This allows one fabric to adhere to another. Also used to bond appliqué fabric pieces to the background or base fabric.

**Contour Spirals:**
Spiraling lines made within any shape, going from the outside edge to the center while following the contour of the shape.

**Couch (verb):**
To place or deposit on the surface. To attach larger threads, yarn, ribbon, or other objects onto the fabric surface using stitches and thread. (This is not a sofa, recliner, or Chesterfield!)

**Cross Hatch (verb):**
To cover a shape with parallel lines that cross obliquely or at right angles.

**Detail (verb):**
To draw in features or details; to draw lines on a shape to define it more clearly; to add minute details to a specific part of a drawing.

**Detail (noun):**
A photograph of an enlarged portion of an artwork that shows the structure and stitchery in a larger size.

**Doodle:**
To draw or scribble loosely, freely, and abstractly without restriction, precision, or feelings of tension.

**Fabriholic:**
A person with an uncontrollable urge to own fabric.

**Frazzled:**
To fray or become frayed or tattered or raveled at the edges.

**Gallumping:**
Leaping or galloping across a surface in lively hops and jumps.

**Gobs:**
A bunch of pieces; a mass; lots; a whole bunch.

**Grumple:**
Gathers, puckers, tucks, and pleats that result from sewing back and forth over fabric many times. Often caused by multiple ziggles.

**Jumper:**
A spring-loaded foot used in free-motion machine stitching. Also called an embroidery foot or darning foot.

**Needle-Run Lace:**
A type of lace made by embroidering fine net with running stitches and filling stitches.

**On/Off Line:**
A line that is drawn to generally follow the

contour of a shape but that wanders inside and outside of the edges of that shape.

**Pizzazz:**
Glamour or vitality.

**Snarly:**
Inclined to growl angrily; snappish; surly; ill-tempered.

**Snippet:**
Small cuts or snips of fabric; a fragment.

**Spirals:**
Lines that go from the outside edge of a circle to the center in one continuous line.

**Squiggles:**
Twisting, squirming, wriggling, meandering lines.

**Stabilizers:**
Iron-on interfacing or bonding or light spray starch used to make a base fabric a bit stiffer and easier to handle. Also used to stiffen the cut edges of small appliqué pieces to reduce fraying and edge disintegration caused by the needle's action.

**Stitch-in-the-Ditch:**
Making quilting stitches that follow a seam line where two fabrics meet.

**Trailing Threads:**
When one motif has been drawn by machine and you wish to move to the next, release the presser foot, trail the threads to the new position, and begin stitching again. Trim trailed thread after stitching is complete.

**Underlap:**
The edge of an appliqué piece that laps underneath another appliqué piece.

**Zig:**
One half of a line that has short, sharp turns or angles; as in zigzag.

**Ziggles:**
Zigzag scribbles used as filling stitches; they may be far apart or close together.

# For Further Reading

Edwards, Betty. *Drawing on the Right Side of the Brain*. (Los Angeles, CA: J.P. Tarcher, Inc., 1979)

Harker, Gail. *Machine Embroidery* (Embroidery Skills Series). (England: Merehurst Press, 1992)

Hargrave, Harriet. *Heirloom Machine Quilting*. (Lafayette, CA: C & T Publishing, 1990)

Hargrave, Harriet. *Mastering Machine Appliqué*. (Lafayette, CA: C & T Publishing, 1991)

Johnson-Srebrow, Nancy. *Featherweight 221: The Perfect Portable*. (Tunkhannock, PA: Silver Star Publishing, 1992)

McGehee, Linda. *Texture With Textiles*. (Self-published, 1991)

Roberts, Sharee Dawn. *Creative Machine Art*. (Paducah, KY: American Quilter's Society, 1992)

Warnick, Kathleen, and Nilsson, Shirley. *Legacy of Lace*. (New York, NY: Crown Publishers, Inc., 1988)

# About the Author

Shirley Nilsson has been creating unique soft pictures using her free-motion straight-stitch technique on the sewing machine since 1969. Born in British Columbia, Canada, she earned a Bachelor's Degree, and later a Master's Degree in Textile Arts from the University of Wisconsin. With her husband and three sons, Shirley has moved many times, living in ten states and Canada. This mobile life has given her the opportunity to know many wonderful friends and to experience the beauty and cultures of many places.

Shirley's professional career includes work as an interior designer, university instructor, art college teacher, extension state housing specialist, and studio artist/designer. She has also created numerous classes and seminars on various artistic techniques and creativity skills. During the last 25 years, Shirley has actively contributed to the growing recognition of fabric art as an exciting and important art form. Her creative machine-drawn works of art have won numerous awards and the loyal patronage of private collectors across the United States and Canada. As a regular contributor to *Creative Quilting* magazine since 1988, she has delighted readers with her nostalgic, whimsical, and realistic style. Shirley has dedicated her life to helping people free the creative spirit that she is confident resides within us all.

Shirley currently lives in Bremerton, Washington, with her husband, cat, and sewing machine. She enjoys phone calls and visits from her three sons and their families, and she has started working on a baby quilt for her third grandchild.

# Other Fine Quilting Books From C & T Publishing

*An Amish Adventure*, Roberta Horton

*Appliqué 12 Easy Ways!*, Elly Sienkiewicz

*The Art of Silk Ribbon Embroidery*, Judith Montano

*Baltimore Album Quilts, Historic Notes and Antique Patterns*, Elly Sienkiewicz

*Baltimore Beauties and Beyond (2 Volumes)*, Elly Sienkiewicz

*The Best From Gooseberry Hill, Patterns for Stuffed Animals and Dolls*, Kathy Pace

*A Celebration of Hearts*, Jean Wells and Marina Anderson

*Christmas Traditions From the Heart*, Margaret Peters

*Crazy Quilt Handbook*, Judith Montano

*Crazy Quilt Odyssey*, Judith Montano

*Design a Baltimore Album Quilt!*, Elly Sienkiewicz

*Dimensional Appliqué—Baskets, Blooms & Borders*, Elly Sienkiewicz

*Friendship's Offering*, Susan McKelvey

*Heirloom Machine Quilting*, Harriet Hargrave

*Imagery on Fabric*, Jean Ray Laury

*Isometric Perspective*, Katie Pasquini-Masopust

*Landscapes & Illusions*, Joen Wolfrom

*The Magical Effects of Color*, Joen Wolfrom

*Mastering Machine Appliqué*, Harriet Hargrave

*Memorabilia Quilting*, Jean Wells

*NSA Series: Bloomin' Creation*, Jean Wells

*NSA Series: Holiday Magic*, Jean Wells

*NSA Series: Hometown*, Jean Wells

*NSA Series: Hearts, Fans, Folk Art*, Jean Wells

*Pattern Play*, Doreen Speckmann

*PQME Series: Milky Way Quilt*, Jean Wells

*PQME Series: Nine-Patch Quilt*, Jean Wells

*PQME Series: Pinwheel Quilt*, Jean Wells

*PQME Series: Stars & Hearts Quilt*, Jean Wells

*Quilts, Quilts, and More Quilts!* Diana McClun and Laura Nownes

*Recollections*, Judith Montano

*Story Quilts*, Mary Mashuta

*3 Dimensional Design*, Katie Pasquini

*A Treasury of Quilt Labels*, Susan McKelvey

*Visions: The Art of the Quilt*, Quilt San Diego

*Whimsical Animals*, Miriam Gourley

For more information write for a free catalog from
C & T Publishing
P.O. Box 1456
Lafayette, CA 94549
(1-800-284-1114)